WELCOME HOME

EMILIE BARNES

WITH *Anne Christian Buchanan*

PHOTOGRAPHY BY MARK LOHMAN

HARVEST HOUSE PUBLISHERS

Eugene, Oregon 97402

WELCOME HOME

Copyright © 1997 by Harvest House Publishers
Eugene, Oregon 97402

Library of Congress Cataloging-in-Publication Data

Barnes, Emilie.
        Welcome Home / Emilie Barnes with Anne Christian Buchanan.
                p.   cm.
        ISBN 1-56507-586-2
        1. Interior decoration—Psychological aspects
                I. Buchanan, Anne Christian. II. Title.
        NK2113.B37 1997
        747—dc21   96-53617
                                                        CIP

Photography by Mark Lohman, 1021 South Fairfax, Los Angeles, CA 90019
Special thanks to Yoli Brogger for her creative work as stylist on the photo shoot.

Design and production by Garborg Design Works, Minneapolis, MN

Scripture quotations are from the Holy Bible, New International Version®. Copyright
© 1973, 1978, 1984 by the International Bible Society. Used by permission of Zondervan
Publishing House.

Manufactured in China
97 98 99 00 01 02 03 04 05 06 / NG / 10 9 8 7 6 5 4 3 2

To all my family, who make our home a
"WELCOME HOME."
Because of them, I've been motivated to make

our home warm, cozy, inviting, and happy.

Thank you, sweet ones, for making me feel it's all

worth it—worth the time, effort, and hard work

needed to build a nest we can all come home to.

C O N T

A Home with Open Arms 6

1. *Make Yourself at Home* 11

SIMPLE SECRETS OF A WELCOMING LIFE
HOUSEWARMINGS: IDEAS FOR AT-HOME LIVING

2. *Instantly at Home* 23

COZY FIRST IMPRESSIONS
HOUSEWARMINGS: IDEAS FOR INVITING
   DOORWAYS AND ENTRANCES

3. *Where the Fireplace Glows* 35

THE WARMTH OF SHARED SPACES
HOUSEWARMINGS: IDEAS FOR WELCOMING LIVING
   ROOMS AND OTHER COMMON AREAS

4. *Company in the Kitchen* 45

THE JOY OF COOKING AND SHARING TOGETHER
HOUSEWARMINGS: IDEAS FOR COMFORTABLE KITCHENS

5. *Merry Occasions & Movable Feasts* . . 55

MAKING MEMORIES WITH SPECIAL CELEBRATIONS
HOUSEWARMINGS: IDEAS FOR AT-HOME CELEBRATIONS

E N T S

6. *Intimate Spaces* 67

THE REST AND ROMANCE OF BED AND BATH
HOUSEWARMINGS: IDEAS FOR BEAUTIFUL PRIVATE ROOMS

7. *Fit for a Princess* 77

THE ROYAL TREATMENT FOR OVERNIGHT GUESTS
HOUSEWARMINGS: IDEAS FOR A WARMHEARTED WELCOME

8. *Always a Place to Play* 87

A HOUSE THAT WELCOMES CHILDREN
HOUSEWARMINGS: IDEAS FOR CHILD-FRIENDLY SPACES

9. *The Fun of Alfresco* 99

BRINGING THE OUTDOORS IN AND THE INDOORS OUT
HOUSEWARMINGS: IDEAS FOR OPEN-AIR LIVING

10. *The Business of Living* 109

CREATING A HOSPITABLE WORK SPACE
HOUSEWARMINGS: IDEAS FOR WELCOMING WORK AREAS

An Evolving Dream 120

A Home with Open Arms

The dusk is fading into darkness as our van exits the highway and makes its way along familiar roads. My tired mind clicks off landmarks: the grocery store, the drugstore, the cemetery, the church. The streetlights are just coming on as we make the left-hand turn onto Rumsey Drive.

Now we really are almost home. It seems like so long since I've been there—more than just the few days I've been away.

I smile to myself. For a person who makes a living talking about home, I don't seem to spend much time there these days. Almost every weekend my husband, Bob, and I are on the road to seminars, conferences,

> *Home! That was what they meant, those caressing appeals, those soft touches wafted through the air, those invisible little hands pulling and tugging, all one way!*
> —**Kenneth Grahame**

and speaking engagements. We live in motels, eat in restaurants, drive down unfamiliar roads.

But not now. Not tonight. We'll spend tonight at home.

Bob slows down the van to turn at our gate. Our big, barn-shaped mailbox looms in the headlights, then slips quietly back into the shadows as we head down the long, curving drive. Past the bench and the avocado trees. Past the bay window and the arching rose arbor and the pond. Past the kitchen window.

I left a lamp burning in the kitchen. Now it beams softly to welcome us.

"Well," I murmur to Bob as I always

do, "there's no place like home."

Wearily we climb down from our seats and begin unloading the van. While we work, our cat Mokie appears from somewhere and strolls toward the car, flicking her long, striped tail just once. Her welcome is reserved, but unmistakable. She's glad we're back.

The key turns willingly in the lock, and the kitchen door swings open. Unbalanced by my bags, I stumble across the threshold, then let my burden sink to the floor.

From every corner, familiar objects seem to smile, to reach out and embrace me. The round oak breakfast-room table sits snug and sturdy under its quilted cover. The pots and pans hang happily in the kitchen where I left them. The fireplace, all clean and laid with wood, waits to spring into flame. The light from the kitchen window caresses me with welcome. The silence is soft, expectant. The very smell is home.

With a peaceful sigh, I head for the bedroom to unpack. There is always work to do when I come home, but even the work welcomes me. My fingers yearn to find a broom and sweep off the porch, to fluff up the pillows, to straighten the pictures.

The house doesn't really need it.

But I do.

I need to make myself, once more, at home.

The Nicest Word in the World

Don't you love that phrase "at home"?

To me it says so much about being cozy in my own nest, about being where I belong, about tending to the most important parts of my life. Being at home means savoring that sense of safety and retreat, even when I'm hard at work. The world may be whizzing by outside, but here I am safe, tranquil, peaceful, productive.

At home.

My favorite days are the ones I spend here, working side by side with my Bob or putting together a snack for our grandchildren or just puttering by myself. And I love to welcome other people in, for being at home to me is closely tied in with making others feel at home.

"Come on in," I love to tell them.

"Come on in. You are very welcome here."

That's why I'm honored when a guest says to me, "I just love to come visit; it's so peaceful here." That sense of peace and rest is what Bob and I have intentionally worked at instilling.

That's why I love to say yes when friends and family ask, "May we have the party (or the meeting or the reception or, occasionally, even the wedding) here?" For many years, Bob and I have found joy in sharing our home and our life with others.

And that's why I was so flattered—if a little surprised—when someone told me, "Staying at your house is just like spending a weekend at a really great bed and breakfast."

I remembered the days and evenings Bob and I had spent in various bed-and-breakfast hideaways here in California and across the nation. I remembered the feeling of beauty and intimacy. The coziness. The sense of somehow being part of the family without being crowded or coerced. The careful planning that made our whole visit seem natural and unforced. I thought of the candles and the flowers and the antiques, the soft music and the good food—as well as the unique and welcoming personality each place displayed to the world.

And I realized that our home really is like a bed and breakfast, but not just for guests. Bob and I have always treasured those qualities in our own lives, and we have tried to build them into our home. From the time we moved into our first tiny apartment—Bob a brand-new teacher, I a child bride of 17—we have worked to make our nest a warm and welcoming kind of place.

We have always wanted a home that holds out open arms to us and to others.

We have wanted a home where guests feel like family, but where family members feel like honored guests.

Isn't that what you want, too?

If so, I invite you to come for a visit in this book, to relax and think and dream about what it means to make a welcoming home—for yourself and others. I want to invite you into my world, my home, and share with you this life I love so much. I want you to think with me about what it is that makes a house seem to open up its arms to family and guests alike.

In more recent years, as Bob and I have traveled across the country, we have learned precious lessons in hospitality from people who have taken us into their own homes. We have experienced the warmth of "at-homeness" in mansions and mobile homes, in sleek, sophisticated apartments and rustic country cabins. And from these wonderful men and women who have shared their homes and their lives with us, we have learned even more about what it takes to make a welcoming, inviting, "homey" home.

How do you achieve these elements in your home and your life? The answers for you are as personal as your house, as unique as your personality, but I hope you will find some ideas and inspiration in this book.

Perhaps you will pick up some tips or be encouraged to make yourself more at home in your own life. Perhaps you will simply enjoy flipping through the pages, thinking with joy and gratitude of your own "at-home" experiences. Or perhaps you will start dreaming about what you would like to do in a someday house.

At any rate, I hope that you will feel very welcome.

Most of all, I hope that you will feel at home.

Go not abroad for happiness. For see
it is a flower that blooms at thy door.

— MINOT J. SAVAGE

Make Yourself at Home

Some homes are places to live. And some homes are restful retreats where you can laugh and love and work and play and dream.

Some homes offer a roof, a kitchen and bath, some bedrooms, and a couple of closets.

And some homes offer shared fellowship, peaceful silence, a comfortable chair, and a vase of flowers.

What makes the difference?

I think it's a matter of making yourself at home.

That's the *true* meaning of the word *homemaking*, and it's the challenge for anyone who wants to live a richer, more comfortable, and more productive home life.

When you make yourself at home, you surround yourself with the people you love, the objects you cherish, the memories that warm you, and the ideas that motivate you. You work to create a nest that helps you be happy and productive, an environment that rests you and renews you. You choose to invest your time, your care, your loving energy to keep your nest clean and warm and welcoming.

From there, it's a natural next step to making other people at home as well. It's just a matter of opening your heart and adjusting your living space to make room for one more person (or a few, or dozens).

And when you have done that, you will have a home with open arms, the kind of welcoming home that enfolds you with comfort and caring.

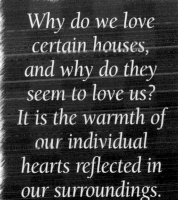

> *Why do we love certain houses, and why do they seem to love us? It is the warmth of our individual hearts reflected in our surroundings.*
>
> —T. H. ROBSJOHN-GIBBINGS

Begin with Your Dreams

How do you begin? Chances are, you've already begun. But you can continue the process of making yourself even more at home with a little bit of thought and a lot of dreaming.

That's where Bob and I began. We started our life together in a tiny apartment—just three small rooms. It would be many years before we finally settled into the home of our dreams, the rustic converted barn where we now live and work. But even then we had a vision of the kind of warm, welcoming, at-home life we wanted.

We knew we wanted it to be comfortable and inviting, the true center of our universe. We knew we wanted a "pulled-together" look, not just a miscellaneous collection of hand-me-downs. We also knew we wanted to share our home and our lives with others.

So we poured our energy into making that little apartment home. Together we sprayed white paint on the old wrought-iron lawn table someone had given us, creating a dainty but sturdy dining table. I sewed pink eyelet curtains for the windows while Bob spray-painted egg cartons to glue on the walls for a "white on white" texture. We had one canvas chair, a box for a lamp table, and an old trunk for a coffee table. But we had wonderful potluck dinner parties in that apartment. We invited our families over. We offered our floor (which was all we had!) for people who needed a place to spend the night.

We felt so wonderfully at home and happy in that first little nest. But we were also full of dreams of the wonderful "someday" house we wanted: a place with cool gardens and rose arbors . . . cozy window seats . . . big, comfortable sofas . . . rustic comfort but formal beauty.

Today, many years later, we are happily at home in that dream house. The gardens and roses and window seats and sofas are a reality. But the sense of "at-homeness" we enjoy here is not all that different from what we knew in that little apartment. In a sense, we have carried our home with us, because we have carried with us our dream of what comfortable, welcoming living would be like.

What is your dream of a welcoming home? What are the desires of your heart regarding the environment where you live and work?

Close your eyes and think about where you love to be. Remember a place you've visited or a place you've lived or a place you've dreamed about. A home where you knew you belonged, where you could work and play and relax and spend time with people you cared about (including your own quiet company). It may be your own home when it's at its best. Or a previous home. Or a place you visited or saw in a magazine. Or a place that exists only in your imagination.

And then ask, What was there specifically about such a place that invited me in and spoke the most enthusiastic welcome?

Your answer, of course, will depend on who you are, what you love, what your needs are.

"I love a home where everything is sparkling and tidy," says one person. "No dishes in the sink, no clothes on the floor, no appliances out on the counter. Nothing to clutter my mind or make me feel guilty."

"I like to see signs that there are people in the house," says another. "I like to see a puzzle out or a book open. I like the kitchen tools hanging where I can use them right away."

"Something to play with," adds a child. "The smell of disinfectant," sighs one overworked mother, "meaning somebody else has been there to clean it!"

Do you see what I mean? The dreams can be lofty or down-to-earth. They will build and change like clouds before a thunderstorm. But if you take the time to dream them, they will work their way inside your heart and find their way inside your environment.

As you dream, and as you plan and build and decorate, gradually you will find yourself more and more at home.

The result, of course, will differ from house to house, from person to person, from taste to taste. And yet I have observed that comfortable, at-home homes share certain common qualities. They subscribe to these few simple guidelines for making guests and family feel cozy, pampered, free to be themselves, free to share life together. These are the principles to keep in mind as you grow your at-home dreams into beautiful, warm, welcoming reality.

Comfortable and Cozy

One vital element of "at-homeness" is simple comfort. No matter how beautiful the decor or how warm the greeting, it's hard to feel at home in a place where you find yourself squirming, shivering, or squinting. No matter how beautiful or how fashionable your living space, it will feel forbidding if there's no comfortable place to sit.

I find that large men are especially sensitive to this element of comfort. They appreciate sturdy, supportive chairs and sofas and live in fear of flimsy wicker and too-short beds. Smaller women are grateful for furniture that is low enough for their feet to touch the floor or for footstools that save their backs by making up the difference. Children love to find a chair or stool that is "just their size." And almost everyone appreciates smooth upholstery, soft cushions, good mattresses, and conveniently placed tables.

In a living area, there should always be a comfortable spot for every member of the family, plus at least one other spot. If your budget is limited, this may have to be a goal rather than an immediate reality. But it is an important goal—one to shape your future decisions.

Bob and I had comfort foremost in mind when we bought the big, soft sofa and chair to furnish our newly redecorated office/sitting room, which we've dubbed the garden room. These squashy, slipcovered treasures practically pat their laps, inviting us to sit and relax. Guests have been known to sigh audibly when they sink in. These new furniture friends—which we recognized as friends the minute we saw them—help make our home more comfortable for us and for the people we bring into our lives.

But there's more to physical comfort, of course, than seating and bedding.

A physically comfortable home is carefully lit. Nobody has to squint, lean, or shade his or her eyes. And nobody has to shiver or stifle, either. A warming fire or a cooling breeze adds a lively sense of coziness, and the air is fresh, not musty. Windows open, doors close, quilts and coverlets are close at hand—and there is always a fan or an extra sweater available.

It doesn't take a redecorating job to provide any of these comforting elements in a living space, although the principle of comfort should guide any redecorating job. Physical comfort is often as much a matter of thoughtfulness and attention as it is of furniture and thermostats. Cushy sofas, glowing fireplaces, convenient lamps, and cozy cushions can all be wonderful, but the real comfort comes from noticing needs and providing for them—making people comfortable in the most literal sense of the word.

It Just Feels Like Home!

But physical comfort isn't the only ingredient that makes a home feel comfortable and welcoming. Even more important than physical comfort is a sense of emotional comfort.

Something feels restful and familiar about a homey home, even if you've never been there before. There are places where you can connect with others, places where you can be alone if you need to. There is a lamp at your shoulder, soft rugs to wiggle your toes in, cozy afghans to snuggle up in.

You somehow feel safe, yet free to be yourself. You feel—there's no other way to put it—at home.

What gives a home these cozy qualities? This is harder to pin down and even more personal than physical comfort. But most of us respond almost unconsciously to certain elements in an environment. They are generally those things that tickle the senses and evoke an emotional response.

Beautiful colors—either cozy and warm or restful and cool—can evoke that sense of emotional comfort. Certain textures of fabric can cuddle and caress. Gentle and familiar sounds—running water, soft music, even the air conditioner—soothe the spirit and offer rest. And smells are especially evocative to most people. Though these responses are intensely personal, certain smells seem to have an almost universal homeward tug, like the yeasty smell of bread baking or the warm scent of soup bubbling on the stove.

A variety of little tricks can do a lot toward filling a home with emotional comfort. A scented candle burning on a dresser or soft pillows on the sofa are inexpensive ways of making a house feel like home. Sachets in the cupboards and the closets can replace musty smells with sweet, evocative ones, and vanilla-scented hand lotion can leave everybody's hands smelling cozily of sugar cookies.

A wool coverlet draped over the back of the sofa or a footstool nestled close to a chair—all these can add that special homelike atmosphere. Even a half-worked puzzle, a needlework project in a basket, or a book with a marker can help give a house that at-home feel.

Surrounded by Beauty

Beauty is not optional in a welcoming, comfortable home. It is as necessary to the spirit as food and clothing are to the body. Not everyone can fill a home with fine art or grace a veranda with an imported fountain, and not everyone will respond to these forms of beauty. And yet a comfortable, at-home house will always contain objects that delight the eye and lift the spirit.

Fortunately, beauty is easy to invite into any home, for beauty has many faces. Beauty can be found in a hand-colored photograph or a hand-stitched quilt, or in shelves lined with bright-hued jelly jars. A pot of graceful ivy can be beautiful, and so can a sweet-potato vine growing in a jar. An heirloom statuette in its place of honor can be beautiful, but so can a shining row of stainless-steel pots.

Even the arrangement of a home can

be beautiful. When furniture and objects, whatever the cost or the style, are combined with care and attention, the result can be warmly beautiful, even if the individual pieces are less than lovely.

What is beautiful to you? What makes you smile in delight or makes your spirit soar? That is the beauty that should surround you in your home, the beauty you should share with all who come to visit.

Seek out beauty in whatever form it speaks to you. Surround yourself with beauty. In the process, you will be creating something truly beautiful as well: a lovely home graced with a happy, welcoming spirit.

Personal Touches

These perceptions, of course, are intensely personal. And that's appropriate, because the most important characteristic of an at-home home is that it reflects the personality of the men and women and children who live there. It is furnished and decorated with a personal touch, and fad or fashion take second place.

I feel immediately at home in houses where people have surrounded themselves with what they love. I like to walk into a house and immediately have a sense of what they read, what they collect, what they like to cook, how they like to spend their time. (This gives me something to talk about, as well.) I enjoy meeting well-behaved pets and seeing evidence that there are children in the home. I feel welcome and comfortable in a room that reflects the owner's personality, and I feel at home in my own rooms because there is so much of me in them.

Our home is filled to overflowing with objects that remind me of who I am and what I love. Clusters of family photos—on a wall of our great room, on a table in the bedroom, on my desk, and on the refrigerator—fill the spaces of our home with smiling, familiar faces. Teacups from my longtime collection retell their stories to me each time I look at them. My mother's secretary and my auntie's crystal build a bridge for my memories. Books and signs and plaques collected on our trips fit together like pieces that make up the puzzle of our lives.

And, of course, these rooms reflect the personality of people I love, as well as my own personality. I see my daughter, Jenny, in the silk flowers and plants that bloom in beautiful profusion around the room. I see my son, Brad, in the uniquely lovely clay pots he made for me in high school, still beautifully holding pencils and keepsakes. The child-sized rocker and the miniature teacups and the toys in the corner remind me of my five grandchildren, each of them gradually putting his or her mark on our house and our hearts.

And, of course, my Bob's personality shines warmly and comfortably from every inch of our house. A single brick was taken from the ruins of the old family home in Anson, Texas. (Its origins are written on the back of the brick.) The antique containers and tools attest to Bob's love of history and his passion for treasure-hunting in antique stores— and they blend together happily with my antique porcelains and silver and lace and linens.

Somehow, it all manages to come together in a homey atmosphere that says, "This is who we are. This is what we love. Please have a seat and let us get to know you, too."

Clean and Comfortable

Bob used to tease me that I would die with a broom in my hand. And it's true that the first thing I usually want to do when I come home from a trip is grab a broom and sweep off the front step. I love that sense of getting my home in order. To me, it's hard to feel comfortable and at home in a house that is dirty, cluttered, or disorganized.

Now this, too, is a personal matter. People differ in the amount of disorder—or order!—they can tolerate. And yet, I am convinced that some sense of organization and order, and yes, cleanliness, are absolutely necessary for most people to feel at home.

I could fill an entire book—in fact, I have filled several books—with hints and ideas for cleaning effectively and keeping clutter under control. That's not really the point here, except to note that a welcoming home is an ordered home. Create a comfortable nest where people you love, including yourself, can work and play and relax and visit without worrying about whether they will step on a metal toy or catch a cold from an unwashed glass or be faced with a discouraging pile of undone chores.

The point of it all, of course, is making yourself and other people at home.

It Takes a Lifetime

It takes a lifetime, this process of making yourself at home.

Homes grow and change just as people do. But these simple secrets of "at-homeness" hold steady through the ongoing homemaking process.

Make yourself comfortable—and create a comfortable environment for yourself and others.

Add the little touches that make a house feel like home.

Surround yourself with beauty.

Surround yourself with *you*.

Create peace by ordering your environment.

Above all else, listen to your dreams of home. Allow them to guide you as you choose where you live, how you furnish your living space, how you decorate, and how you offer hospitality.

Allow your dreams to guide you as you learn to make yourself and others happily at home.

Housewarmings

❧ Don't let a tiny budget keep you from dreaming. Keep a notebook of ideas you like, tips from magazines, pictures, instructions, etc. When you do have the money, you'll know what you want to do.

❧ If you want your living space to be comfortable and welcoming to everyone who lives there, include everyone in the process of planning and decorating. You may need to alter your dream of a dainty wicker-and-chintz sitting room to accommodate your husband's dreams of a deep leather easy chair, but the result of your collaboration will be more comfortable and welcoming to everyone.

❧ Break free from the mental prison of "it has to match." There's no law that says you have to have a chest of drawers that matches your headboard or a chair upholstered the same as a sofa. A variety of designs can add liveliness, warmth, and individuality to your home.

❧ It's no fun to be a lone-ranger homemaker. Ask a friend to help you in the process of choosing fabric, hanging pictures, even refinishing furniture—then return the favor.

❧ If you love a custom look but don't have a custom budget, consider a "part-designer" approach. Use a professional to help you procure the right basic pieces—perhaps a sofa, chair, and rug—then decorate the rest of the room on your own.

❧ If you have a chair or a piece of furniture that everyone fights over, why not buy another? If everyone avoids a certain chair and you are not attached to it for sentimental or decorative reasons, get rid of it. Life's too short not to be comfortable at home.

❧ Handmade items—wall hangings, pillows, wood carvings, even dolls—are wonderful for creating a warm, personal look. If you don't have the time or the inclination to make it yourself, try craft sales and consignment shops, or commission a handmade item from a gifted friend.

- Your children's art can be an untapped source of decorating treasure in your home. Frame a series of crayon drawings in matching craft-store frames and hang as a group on your kitchen or hallway wall.

- Use items from your collections as a decorating motif to give your home that distinctive touch of you and a sense of unity. In our house, for instance, items from our collections of teacups and teapots, roosters, ducks, and antique scales appear throughout the house.

- Baskets, quilts, musical instruments, tools, and collections can have wonderful design possibilities. Instead of stowing them away, consider hanging them from the wall or ceiling where they are easily accessible for use but also decorative.

- The 15-minute principle can do a lot toward keeping your house orderly and welcoming without your becoming bogged down in housekeeping chores. Break down necessary tasks into 15-minute increments and spread them throughout the day. Unclutter the living room while waiting for your daughter to get ready for Girl Scouts. Or clean out a drawer while you talk on the phone.

- For a touch of old-fashioned charm, try "dressing" your house for the change of seasons. For summer, take down the drapes and slipcover your furniture in light, bright colors. For winter, pull out your cozy rugs, heavy drapes, and other cold-weather friends.

The charm of a house, like the charm of a person,
is an outward manifestation of inward grace.

—**Emily Post**

GOD BLESS OUR HOME

Instantly at Home

Your mama always told you that first impressions count. But if you've always heard that as a daunting warning, embrace it now as a warm opportunity. With a little thought and a little caring, you can have a home that makes guests and family alike feel instantly at home.

Where do you begin?

In a sense, you begin at the door, or even at the curb.

More accurately, though, you begin with a hospitable heart.

You begin with a willingness to share your life, to make space in your plans for friends, family, and strangers.

From there, it's just a matter of a little planning and a little creativity to make your welcome immediately obvious.

> *We welcome you most cordially. We welcome you most regally.*
>
> —FRANK BAUM

A whimsical mailbox by the driveway, for instance, can say a happy hello to anyone who approaches. (Ours is an oversized barn, custom-made to hold our large volume of mail and to play off our Barnes name.)

A curving walkway dotted with lamps or visited by shy lawn animals can lead the way to welcome.

A bright banner hanging in the apartment hallway can announce, "This is the right place—and we want you in it!"

Best of all, the sight of you standing at the door with a glass of warm cider or cold iced tea gives the unmistakable message: "You're welcome here. We're thrilled to see you. Please come in and make yourself at home."

A Custom-Tailored Welcome

However it is expressed, the best kind of first impression is a personal one. It reflects your tastes, speaks clearly of your caring. If possible, it is directed specifically to the person arriving.

One of the most charming and surprising welcomes I ever experienced was at the home of my good friend Donna Otto. We had met many times and then shared several speaking engagements before I ever went to visit in her Scottsdale, Arizona, home. Donna picked me up at the airport and drove me home with her, winding through the desert landscaping to her garage. The automatic door opener whirred, and we drove inside. And there on the wall of the garage, right next to the kitchen door, was a big blackboard with the words, "Welcome, Emmy."

What a wonderful, creative greeting! Donna had thought ahead about how I would be entering her home, then she had arranged her greeting to match. I learned later that the little chalkboard, which once belonged to her daughter, is a family message center where she and her family leave notes, reminders, and "I love yous" throughout the day.

Bob and I have adapted Donna's idea to our own place. We placed a little chalkboard right outside our kitchen door, which is where most of our informal visitors come. Bob especially loves to change our chalkboard greeting to suit whomever we expect. The week prior to our granddaughter's recent birthday, that little chalkboard announced, "Christine is almost 13." On the big day it exulted, "Christine is 13 today!" And, of course, we have put out similar greetings for our other grandchildren and other beloved guests.

Another welcoming touch we are very fond of outside our house is the bench beside our door. (We have another one up near the gate, and yet another by a footpath under some trees.) To me, a bench just calls out to friends to sit down and relax a bit. It's a little like a porch swing, which I think is one of the world's great inventions—along with big, shady front porches.

A chair, a bench, a rocker, a swing—there's just something in the visual symbolism that invites people to "set a spell." But whatever greets your guests when they approach your drive or your walk or your steps, let it be personal and cheerful. Let it be as beautiful as possible. And don't underestimate the welcoming power of a neatly manicured lawn and well-swept, neatly edged sidewalks. Don't discount the appeal of a freshly painted, cobweb-free doorway.

A House with a Smiling Face

A welcoming home, in other words, looks well-tended and lovingly cared for. It presents a smiling, friendly face to the world.

Even if you love the studied untidiness of an English country garden or the private loveliness of a Spanish courtyard-style home, even if you have chosen to landscape your home in native plants or have not had time to grow trees or plant flower beds, there are ways to arrange the outside so that the house looks welcoming. A fresh coat of paint does wonders. A pot of mums or an ornamental sconce by the outside wall softens the barricade effect of a gated property. And guests will certainly feel more at home if they don't have to dodge potholes, duck under branches, maneuver around cracks in the sidewalk, or step over weeds, lawn toys, or forgotten lawn implements!

I am especially grateful to my Bob for the careful and loving way he tends and improves the outside of our house and grounds. Although our home has always been a shared joy and a joint responsibility, he is the one largely responsible for the smiling face our home turns to the world.

It was Bob who thought of the long, curving drive that leads people gently around to the front of the house instead of dumping them unceremoniously at the door. He is the one who built and keeps improving the grounds with their lawns, pond, and garden. He is the one who drew on his farm background and interests to decorate chosen areas with fascinating old farm implements and, especially, the wonderful old wagon that we bank with hay or fill with plants. Bob personally built the lovely rose arbor that arches over our front entranceway, engulfing our spring visitors with the intoxicating fragrance of climbing pink and yellow roses. And he is the one who conceived the idea for the rustic tree house that draws young visitors like a magnet.

My Bob is especially sensitive to the ways that the outside of a house can help guests and family feel comfortable and welcome and delighted with beauty. And his efforts make me feel more at-home, too. I love to come home from my errands, negotiate the graceful curve of the driveway, and drive past the serene pond as I pull up in front of our garage. I love to pick a flower or two or a spray of ivy to carry inside with me. I love to watch the faces of our guests as they enjoy the tree-shaded paths or gaze out over the pond or lean over to sniff the roses. And I love to be able to lean on our Dutch doors to greet them as they walk up.

An Open-Door Policy

That's where my part of our home's first-impression welcome comes in. People who arrive at our house can choose the front door or the kitchen door (most of our friends enter through the kitchen). But if I am home, chances are I'll have the top part of each door—or the whole door—open to say, "Come in."

Installing those Dutch doors on both our entrances was the first change we made when we moved into this home, and we had this kind of door on our previous home as well. I love the way Dutch doors let in the breeze and the sunshine while keeping small children in and neighborhood pets out.

My mama was the one who taught me the welcome of an open door. During the years after my father's death, when we lived in three rooms behind Mama's little dress shop, she always left the shop door open. In those pre-air-conditioning days, that door seemed to beckon customers in.

Many years later, when Mama lived in an efficiency apartment in a senior-citizen high-rise, she continued her open-door policy. It was known throughout the building that when Irene "cracked her door," leaving it open just a little bit, anybody was welcome to come in and share a cup of tea.

Dutch doors are *my* way of saying welcome. If a literal open-door policy is not practical for you, there are many other ways to make your entranceway friendly and personable.

Your front door itself, for example, can say hello with remarkable eloquence. Even if you live in an apartment building with rows of look-alike doors, you can make your personal entrance look unique and welcoming. An antique knocker. A little message board. A seasonal decoration such as a shock of Indian corn or a bouquet of sunflowers or a Christmas stocking. Wind chimes or mellow door chimes. A whimsical animal statue with a bow around its neck. A classic welcome mat. Any of these can say, "Someone's home," as well as beckon visitors and family inside.

It goes without saying that guests should find it easy to announce themselves. Does the doorbell work? Can a knock be easily heard inside? Is it clear what visitors should do to let you know they've arrived?

Here is where a touch of whimsy can really help. A little wreath around a defunct doorbell with a carefully lettered sign—"Ouch! I'm broken. Please use the knocker" or "Please come around back; all our friends use the kitchen door"—can save a visitor that moment of hesitation or frustrated minutes of fruitless knocking.

The First Thing You See

And once the door is open, the first-impression welcome remains just as important. In fact, what greets the eye and ear and nose upon entering a house will do a lot toward shaping a person's experience of the house.

The first thing that meets the eye when people are entering your home (and the second thing, too) should be beautiful, homey,

inviting—or all three.

The basics should be present, of course: a place to wipe feet, a place to hang coats. But beyond that, the entranceway sets the mood and sends a message about the whole house.

A neat foyer with a shiny floor, sparkling mirror, and a closet for hats and coats says, "This house is orderly and peaceful."

A sunlit entrance hall graced by a hanging quilt and a winsome collection of teddy bears sends a clear message that whimsy and play are a part of your life.

A cozy apartment living room with plump cushions, soft music, and lots of candles says, "Come right on in and let us get to know you."

And, of course, the smell of something wonderful on the stove sends an unmistakable welcome message to anyone who steps over the threshold.

I know of more than one person who has managed to sell her house quickly by popping a loaf of bread dough into the oven before prospective buyers showed up. And I used that trick with great success once when our home was part of a home tour. The morning of the tour, I simply popped a ham in the oven to bake slowly. By the time the first people arrived, that ham was beginning to smell delectable. And by the time evening rolled around, our stomachs were really starting to growl. But that was all right because we had invited friends to come by for supper. They all brought accompaniments for the ham—bread, potato salad, beans—and we had a wonderful feast. Later, we learned that our home was the talk of the tour!

Cooking is not the only source of wonderful smells, though it's one that most people love. Flowers, fragrance candles, and potpourri can also scent the air deliciously. One of my favorite tricks is to pull out a can of Christmas potpourri spray whenever I see a car coming down the drive. It just takes a second, and that delicious aroma of pine or cinnamon seems to put people in an instant holiday mood—even in July.

A Welcoming Message for Everyone

When I speak of welcoming first impressions, I'm not talking just about the front hall or foyer. If you or your family and friends usually enter by a different door than guests do, try to make that entrance beautiful, too. With a little organization and care, even a mudroom can be kept tidy and pleasing to the eye.

Bob and I almost always use our kitchen door because that is the door closest to the garage. But I also like to come in that way because the kitchen door opens directly onto one of my favorite rooms in the house: the little breakfast room next to the kitchen. This is the room where we eat many of our meals. It's the room where little children love to play by the fire, where our antique Hoosier cabinet and an old oak wall phone proudly preside, and where a little round oak table sits to temporarily relieve us of bags and parcels.

Precisely because this is the room that always greets us first, we have filled it with things we love. And we try to resist the urge to make the breakfast room a dumping ground. It takes just a tiny bit of extra effort to pick the bags back up and move them to their proper home. And then that cozy, cheerful little room is once more ready to welcome the next person who steps inside.

I think it's vital to remember always that your home's welcome is not just for visitors. Don't underestimate the power of these little touches to make your own family feel at home. A welcoming, at-home greeting should always extend first of all to the people who live there, yourself included. Even those little imperfections you hardly notice anymore—the muddy boots by the doorway, the bag of garbage waiting by the door, the broken hinge that reaches out to snag sweaters—can be little irritants that drag your spirit down.

If you live alone, it's even more important to create a pleasing first impression. In a sense, your home itself is what welcomes you after a long day. Doesn't it make sense to make the welcome as warm as possible? Something as simple as a light turned on by a timer, a radio playing soft music, or dinner in a Crockpot can soften that feeling of coming home to a dark, empty house or apartment. A few minutes of straightening in the morning can take away the stress of coming home to a house full of things to do.

It all starts, remember, with making yourself feel at home. The first place to do that is the place where you walk in the door.

And don't forget that people go out of doors and entranceways as well as into them. Final impressions can be important, too. I like to have something hanging by the door *on the inside* that says a friendly farewell—perhaps a plaque with a poetic blessing, a mirror to double-check hair or makeup, or just a pretty decoration that you don't see until you leave. There's no reason you can't hang a wreath on the inside of the door, just to say a smiling good-bye.

A Personal Touch—Coming & Going

The best possible way to greet family and visitors alike is literally with your open arms, or at least with your smiling presence. Whenever possible, I like to be there to meet our guests face-to-face as they park at the curb or climb the stairs or come up the walk. There's just something special about an in-person greeting that says, "I really mean it—you're welcome here."

Our dear friends Jim and Barbara DeLorenzo like to take this idea of a face-to-face hello even further. They like to sit on their top step with a cool drink, smilingly waiting for their guests to drive up. More eloquently than any words, their eager, welcoming presence says, "We just can't wait to be with you!"

Taking our cue from Jim and Barbara, Bob and I will sometimes wait for our guests at the top of our driveway, relaxing on the bench under the avocado tree. As soon as we see a car approach our gate, we stand up to say hello, then follow the car down the driveway. Then we can all go in and enjoy the house's welcome together.

There are other ways to achieve that wonderful "I can't wait for you" feeling. If you have children, for instance, you can send them outside to watch for the new arrivals, then ask them to bring the guests inside and take their coats. A spouse or housemate can perform the same welcoming job. Or at the very least, you can put out a sign or banner that says "Welcome."

It's not hard to add a personal touch

that makes guests and family feel instantly at home. Just a few simple gestures can do wonders for making newcomers feel special and pampered.

I've watched my daughter, Jenny, do this millions of times with wonderful, welcoming grace. No matter how busy she is with preparations, when guests arrive (even if they're family), she takes the time to "nest" them. She greets them at the door, takes their coats, leads them to a chair, and makes them comfortable with a drink at their elbow and something to nibble on. Sometimes she will seat them at her breakfast bar with a cup of tea and a plate of cookies. Other times she will settle them comfortably in the living room with a bowl of chips and a cold glass of something good before going back to finish her preparations. When guests leave, she gathers everyone in the house to walk them out to the car and see them off.

People never visit Jenny's house without feeling loved and welcome. They never leave without feeling she's sorry to see them go. The first impressions and the last impressions in Jenny's home reflect her beautiful heart of hospitality. She says she learned it growing up, but I know she is constantly teaching me.

This kind of hospitality isn't just for company. You might be amazed at what happens when you take the time to greet your own family with that special "I'm excited to see you" welcome. Why not stroll out to meet your weary spouse at the end of a hard day or walk to the bus stop to greet your children as they get off the bus? If everyone comes home together, why not have snacks and drinks in the refrigerator for a little family "happy hour" before the evening starts?

The same applies to everyday good-byes. Instead of a distracted peck or a shouted good-bye, occasionally go for a big hug and a personal escort out the door. Every once in a while, a little wrapped gift or a note slipped into a backpack or a briefcase can start a day off with an extra bit of sunshine.

Coming and going, these special, personal gestures express the spirit of hospitality that makes guests and family alike feel instantly at home. The unmistakable message in your decor, in your actions, and in your heart is the message of welcome: "I really am glad you came. And I just can't wait until you come back."

HOUSEWARMINGS

IDEAS FOR INVITING DOORWAYS AND ENTRANCES

- Shortly before your guests arrive or your family comes home, take a minute to create a serene atmosphere. Clear the clutter in the living room or entry hall, light candles, put on soft music. And call a moratorium on problems and "discussions" for the next 30 minutes. If you live alone, give yourself half an hour of rest before tackling the evening chores.

- Keep a guest book in your home for visitors to sign. You can buy one in a stationery store or have your children make one.

- Your foyer or entrance hall is a great place for a "love wall." Group all the little plaques and pictures people have given you as gifts into a decorative reminder of how much people care. Or use that space for a gathering of candid family photos.

- Take a poll among the members of your family: What one thing about a house makes you feel that it's clean and comfortable and welcoming? You may be surprised at the answers you receive! But use those answers as a guide to what you should concentrate on when time is short. If a clean sink makes your husband feel comfortable and welcome, let the bathroom go, but clean the sink!

- For an old-fashioned welcoming touch, try painting your door a bright red, a glossy green, or a shiny black.

- If your time or enthusiasm for gardening is limited, choose only one small area at the front of your house for something green or growing: one rosebush next to the door, a single clematis vine climbing the mailbox pole, or a potted plant on the porch.

- The main entrance to your home is a good place to celebrate the changing seasons. Your front door can always say "Welcome" with a May basket, a fall arrangement of Indian corn, or a green wreath for Christmas. A simple grapevine wreath can be wound with different-colored ribbons and bouquets of seasonal plants, flowers, and leaves. Or install a flagpole from which you fly multicolored banners that announce the season.

~ Don't neglect the entranceway to your apartment or office. If regulations permit, post a friendly greeting or hang a banner or bulletin board. Not only will guests feel more welcome, but fellow residents also will have their day brightened.

~ If you are expecting a pint-sized guest, prepare a welcome bag or basket. A brown paper bag will do just fine. Write his or her name on the outside and put in a welcome note plus a small gift: an apple, a pack of gum, crayons and some paper, or a little book. Leave by the front door for your little visitor to discover.

~ Before leaving on a trip, set aside half an hour before you leave to straighten the house so it will greet you with serenity instead of clutter.

~ If you live alone and travel often on business, plug a radio and a lamp into an outlet controlled by a light switch near the door. One flip of the switch, and your homecomings will be celebrated by light and music.

~ Periodically try to look at your house with fresh eyes. Go out on the front step, ring your own doorbell, and walk inside. Look around you as if you had never seen the place before. What catches your eye? What do you like? What detracts from the welcoming, at-home feeling?

By wisdom a house is built, and through understanding it is established; through knowledge its rooms are filled with rare and beautiful treasures.

—PROVERBS 24:3,4

Where the Fireplace Glows

THE WARMTH OF SHARED SPACES

This is the room where the home fires burn the brightest, but the fireplace is optional!

Yes, a flickering fireside adds an irresistible, cozy glow. But even without the fireplace, this room is the center of warmth, the gathering place where family members come together gladly and where guests quickly become one of the family. Call it the living room, the den, the family room—the name doesn't really matter. It could be the corner of an efficiency apartment or even, in the right climate, a front porch. Regardless of what you call it, though, every home needs one—a place for people to "set a spell" and share their lives.

> *Blest be that spot, where cheerful guests retire to pause from toil, and trim their ev'ning pair, and every stranger finds a ready chair.*
>
> —**OLIVER GOLDSMITH**

For us, that room is our great room, the spacious central chamber that spreads out before you after you walk through the door. Something about this space seems to call out to anyone who walks by: "Come on in. Sit down. Let's spend some time together."

It was this room, in fact, that sold me on our home in the first place. I love our great room because it is a living room in the truest sense. We *live* here—we come together in this room to share our lives and share each other's company.

It is here that we entertain guests, gather for family discussions, or sit and talk or watch TV. An open breakfast counter connects it to the kitchen, so I can cook and still be part of the action. The massive fireplace toasts our toes and warms our spirits on cool evenings. A big, cheerful window lets the sunlight pour in. There is space for children to play, for adults to talk, for Bob to read or watch a football game in his big, green leather chair, for me to curl up on the couch with my favorite magazines.

A Room of Stories

And there is plenty of room for memories here, too—a good thing, because our great room is filled with them. Every object around us tells a story about the events in our lives that have made us who we are.

The faces of people I love smile at me all around this room—sometimes in person, sometimes in memory, and always in the form of photographs that populate every table and hang from the walls as well. One table holds photographs of women in our family—from the grandmother I never knew to granddaughter Christine. Another table holds pictures of Bob's parents and mine. A wall arrangement of black-and-white shots, new and old, shows the faces of people I love in a strikingly different light.

I don't really need the pictures, though, to summon the memories. Just being here tells me stories of the moments in our lives.

Our son, Brad, proposed to his Maria here—lying flat on his back, deathly ill with the measles. She had assumed all the flowers and balloons that filled the room were sickroom offerings, until he pulled the ring from under his pillow. So now, when I look around this room, it retells me a story about roses and balloons and measles . . . and love.

We've had parties in this room, too. Birthdays. Gatherings of loved ones. Even a wedding or two. An endless parade of Thanksgivings and Christmases, the whole room spangled with lights and fragrant with greenery. Hanukkah celebrations, too, that represented a rediscovery of my Jewish heritage and a reconciliation with family members who had long resented my embracing a different faith.

The special moments, the special memories sparkle when I gaze around the room. But the everyday moments are equally precious. All around me march a priceless procession of ordinary moments that have defined our ongoing life together. Mothers nursing babies. Children snuggled in their blankies, watching TV or listening to a story. Bob and I close together on the couch, making plans for our next business venture or our next landscaping project. Even the painful moments—the difficult discussions, the frustrating arguments, the times of silence and worry—are part of the memory glow that makes this room home to me.

Not Just for Company

This memory room is a family room. It is also the room where we welcome guests and strangers into our midst and make them part of us. We do not have a special receiving room reserved just for "company." When you come to visit us, you live with us in the warmth of our shared spaces.

I don't mean that we shouldn't honor guests as special. A visitor should be celebrated, treated always with joyful, even gleeful hospitality. But we should treat ourselves and our families that way, too. We honor each other, and then we include guests as part of that honored company. We welcome them around the family hearth, but we also make sure that the family hearth is a clean, cozy, beautiful place to be.

I have never liked the idea of maintaining a separate living room where the drapes are kept drawn to protect the upholstery, where children are not allowed to sit on the furniture, where the beautiful objects and "good" furniture gather dust while the family rooms are filled with shabby, old chairs and "childproof" knickknacks. How can such a situation feel welcoming to either family or guests, when the family is deprived of the beauty of treasured objects and guests are deprived of the warmth of the family hearth?

How much better to create a living area that is warm, beautiful, well-lived-in but also well-kept, and that welcomes family and company alike?

Why not share your memories, your comfort, your hearth with those who come to visit?

And why not give your best and most beautiful to the people who use the house the most?

Arranged for Welcome

How you arrange your common areas and how you choose the spaces where people will gather depends on you, your budget, and your floor plan. In a small house or apartment, you may have only one choice: The sofa will go here and nowhere else, the bookshelves must go where there is wall space, and so on. A larger home may offer more options and demand more decisions: Do you need a separate music room, sewing room, library, or recreation room?

But regardless of your resources, this basic principle of maintaining an inviting hearth space for family and friends can guide you in creating welcoming rooms that invite people to sit and share their lives.

I personally like an open, flowing living space, where the roles of kitchen and dining room and living room sometimes overlap. When I cook, I like to be close to my family, and I love to eat in front of the fire. I enjoy being able to see into my bedroom or to hear the grandchildren play in the loft overhead and the fountain trickling outside in the courtyard.

You may prefer (or your home may demand) a more formal arrangement. Perhaps you enjoy having the kitchen separate from the living room so that you can ignore the dirty dishes for a little while after dinner. Perhaps you love the look of a formal dining room for meals, a quaint little morning room for tea, a dreamy little library nook—a series of beautiful little surprises to discover and enjoy one at a time.

But even if you are fortunate enough to have myriad living areas, the same principle still holds. Instead of having one room for show and one for family, why not establish *two* warm, beautiful living areas?

Each room should be wonderful and welcoming to the people who live in the home.

And each room should be wonderful and welcoming to the people you invite into your lives.

There may be reasons to separate living spaces according to mood or decor: her dainty floral sun room, for instance, and his rich-looking, leather-bound library. It may also make sense to have separate spaces for different kinds of shared activities so that one person can play the piano while another watches TV, or so that one person can read while another exercises.

But in this day of increasing separation and isolation, isn't it time we rediscovered the art of togetherness, of sharing space and time and memories together?

So many family activities can coexist in the same room—perhaps better than you think. Children can play quietly on the rug while Grandma knits or reads a magazine.

Dad and Mom can file tax receipts while a guest reads a magazine. Sister can practice the piano while the rest of the family actually listens or sings along.

Sharing the Area

Besides memories, what are the essentials of an at-home living area?

There must be a comfortable place to sit, perhaps a comfortable place to stretch out, with plenty of cushions or pillows. A carpet or warm rugs provide the kind of "soft floor" that children love and adults appreciate.

Because this is a place where people can relax, it should also be relatively low maintenance, a place where spills can be tolerated and feet don't always have to stay on the floor. This should also be a beautiful space. Your primary gathering place should be filled with what you love, whether it's antique flour mills or handmade kaleidoscopes or model airplanes.

Of course, it will be filled with what your family loves as well, for this is shared space. That means that the needs and tastes of everyone who will be using the room must be taken into account.

In this room, in other words, my florals must coexist with Bob's leather. My dolls must live with his antique store signs. My lace curtains must harmonize with his farm tools.

In our experience, at least, this process of merging our tastes into a beautiful whole has been a wonderful adventure. We have found that our tastes marry well, and many of our loves coincide: the paintings, the collections of little barns, the antique armoires, the Amish quilts. The key is love, respect, and sometimes a willingness to put up with something that just isn't "you" in favor of a total effect of "we."

Activities, too, may need to be synchronized in a shared living area.

What do the people in your family love to do: play music, watch sports, wrestle on the floor? Your living room will be warmer and everyone will feel more at home if you make space for those activities to take place.

If you love to exercise in front of the TV or if certain music on the stereo moves you to spontaneous outbreaks of dance, make sure your coffee table and extra chairs can be easily moved. If pets are part of your life, the dogs and cats should have a comfortable place to curl up. If yours is a "crafty" family, there's no reason you can't enjoy your hobbies in the living area. A model airplane can take shape happily on a card table in the corner. With a sewing basket and a good light, the family seamstress can do handwork while watching TV or talking.

And living rooms provide a perfect setting for whole-family activities. For many years when our family was young, Friday nights were family night, when we would pop corn, play games, or just talk and spend time together. Such gatherings can be wonderful, warm uses of a living room.

Why not read a book together in installments, letting Tolkien or Dickens or Winnie the Pooh draw you closer in beauty and laughter?

Why not let each person choose a video and have an all-day family film-festival marathon?

Why not sing, accompanied by anything from oatmeal-box drums to a junior pianist to a karaoke machine?

Why not play charades . . . or look at photograph albums . . . or even talk!

Being Together or Being Alone

The whole point of a living room is to be at home together. If you set up the space to make room for togetherness, people will be more likely to gather there.

Little touches can make a big difference.

The way the furniture is arranged, for example, can tell a lot about your priorities and your at-home spirit.

Does the furniture "turn its back" to a newcomer or block the view of the fire? Are there comfortable groupings for conversation?

Does every seat have an adequate lighting source and a place to put down drinks? Is there room to move without knocking things over?

Perhaps most important, where is the TV? Many living rooms or family rooms these days are set up with every chair pointed in the direction of the TV. No wonder our society has a problem with TV addiction. No wonder family time often disintegrates into merely staring at the tube together.

Where to put the TV, therefore, is not just a decorating issue; it's also a question of family priorities. With a little experimentation, you can help play down the TV's role in your shared life. My friend Yoli accomplished this by placing the TV on a high stand in the corner of a room. It's visible from most places, but not an integral part of the furniture grouping. We've tried to do the same thing by placing our large TV low and in a corner. I've seen some wonderful and inexpensive armoire-type cabinets with doors that close. And I know some people who keep their TV on a wheeled cart in the closet, ready to roll out for special occasions, but safely stowed during ordinary family evenings.

If space permits, I like to fill a living space with several separate little groupings, not only the traditional gathering of sofas and chairs around a coffee table. My mother's wing chair sits over by a little table with a lamp—a nice place to sit and write a letter. A gathering of child-sized chairs and toys near the fire invites small people to make themselves at home. Bob's chair with its oversized hassock is comfortably arranged near his magazine rack and a cheery floor lamp—a wonderful place to read, nap, and yes, watch TV. Several little tables hold groups of photos and conversation pieces. Even the breakfast bar with its high stools offers a separate area for work or conversation. It's Bob's favorite

place to read and drink coffee in the mornings.

And we have sofas and coffee tables, too—big ones to hold our big family and the many people we love.

But the living room and its furniture don't need to be big to be welcoming and inviting. All the room really needs is a comfortable space for everyone to sit, and then one or two places more.

I've felt thoroughly welcome and at home in tiny efficiency apartments with furniture crammed wall to wall, or in new, big houses with barely a stick of furniture. I've felt comfortable in homes where children and teenagers were constantly coming in and out the doors, and in quiet, serene homes where one man or woman has lived alone for many years.

What matters, you see, is not the size of the room or the number of people who share the space, but the warmth of the welcome to resident and guest alike.

What matters is the memories, with the stories attached.

What matters is being able to sit and talk and play and share our lives.

What matters is that warm fireside glow—with or without the fire.

If the living room is warm, the house will always feel like home.

Housewarmings

IDEAS FOR WELCOMING LIVING ROOMS
AND OTHER COMMON AREAS

- If you are lucky enough to have a fireplace, make that the focus of your room. Invest in useful but beautiful tools, attractive boxes for wood, even utensils for cooking over the fire. In warm-weather months, clean the fireplace carefully and fill the space with green plants, an ornamental fan, even a family of teddy bears in a basket.

- There's something about a rocking chair that encourages people to sit and talk, and the rocking motion is good for your circulation. Hold out for a rocker that's truly comfortable.

- Rotating your pictures not only keeps a room fresh, but it can also cut down on sun damage. Any picture that is exposed to sunlight even part of the day should be rotated out of that damaging environment.

- Look to your personal past as a source of making your home look cozy and homey. A favorite stuffed toy, a framed picture of yourself with your grandmother, even your silver baby cup—any memento that touches you with a cozy glow—can also make your home look warmer and cozier.

- Photos and vacation souvenirs have wonderful potential for making your house feel like home. I read about one woman who keeps seasonal pictures of her family in a drawer and puts them out in the proper season: Christmas pictures at Christmas, vacation pictures in the summer, and so forth. Her home is like a changing seasonal gallery.

- A card table with matching chairs is one of the best investments you can make in informal sharing. It will last for years, can be easily stored, and presents a billion opportunities for informal sharing in your living area and all over the house. Set up in a corner, it holds a puzzle in progress. Next to the hearth and draped with a quilt, it's just the thing for fireside dining. The chairs offer extra seating for impromptu gatherings. If all else fails, you can always play games on it!

- Discover the beauty of slipcovers to extend the life of your furniture and reduce the fear of stains from comfortable living. Whether you rely on a simple throw from a discount store or a custom-designed set of covers, look for washable fabric and cozy colors.

- You can almost never have too many pillows. For a quick change of mood, tie throw pillows up like a package in lengths of fabric, or tack tea towels to the front of several cushions.

- If you have a futon, you can instantly change the look of your room with a fitted sheet. Just slip the sheet over the futon like it was the mattress on a bed. If the sheet comes as part of a set, use the flat sheet and pillowcases for creating matching pillows, tablecloths, or floor cushions.

- Make sure there is something warm near the sofa or chair for snuggling: an afghan, a quilt, or a blanket. When not in use, stack the covering beneath a table, tuck it away in a trunk, or simply drape it over the arm of a chair.

- Many people find a puzzle irresistible, and much fun can be shared around a puzzle table. If you can stand the slight untidiness, leave a half-worked puzzle out for anyone to go by and work on until it's finished. Or build a puzzle board with a lid that can be tucked away, puzzle intact, or pulled out to work on.

- Instead of a traditional lamp table, try stacking a series of sturdy wooden trunks or stenciled packing boxes. An old trunk also serves beautifully for both coffee table and storage.

Live in harmony with one another.

—Romans 12:16

Company in the Kitchen

THE JOY OF COOKING AND SHARING TOGETHER

Sometimes I think that I was born in a kitchen.

At least, my earliest happy memories all seem to be kitchen memories.

In my mind's eye I can see myself, a tiny girl of four or five, perched on a countertop amid mounds of chopped vegetables, countless bottles and jars of spices, dustings of flour. I loved to watch my father as he cooked.

My father was a creative, temperamental Viennese chef. Orphaned at a young age, he had been raised in the kitchens of the palace of Vienna, and the kitchen was his native habitat. In the early 1940s, after he came to America, he worked for Fox Studios in Hollywood. Many of the old-time movie stars—

Afterwards, they always had tea in the kitchen, much the nicest room in the house.

—FLORA THOMPSON

including Clark Gable, Lana Turner, Mario Lanza, and Betty Grable—joined in standing ovations for my father's lavish buffets.

I remember shared times in the kitchen with my father, warm times—time spent together as the ingredients flew and the aromas mingled and wonderful dishes were created.

Ever since those days, it seems, my happiest times have involved preparing and serving food in the company of people I love. I treasure that legacy of memory, just as I treasure my father's stainless-steel ladle, his chef's knife, and his wonderful recipe for olive-oil dressing. And I love an open kitchen where more happens than just meal preparation. To me, the kitchen is the place in the home where many blessings begin: the blessing of nourishment, the blessing of fellowship, the blessing of creativity, the blessing of shared meals and shared lives.

Years ago, someone gave me the plaque that expresses that reality succinctly: "No matter where I serve my guests, it seems they like my kitchen best."

That's certainly true for me. And I'm always happy to have company here in the kitchen. It's not proprietary space. I think of it as the heart of the home, where good food begins and good fellowship happens.

And if you spend any time in my home, chances are you'll be spending at least part of it in my kitchen.

A Place You Love to Be

Our current kitchen is spacious and convenient, with lots of pantry and cupboard space. I love its barnwood paneling, its glassed-in shelves, its deep pantry, its handy hangers for pots and pans.

But I don't have to have a perfect facility to be at home in the kitchen.

I have enjoyed cooking and sharing in many homes and many kitchens, and I have learned that even the smallest of them can be organized, efficient, and inviting.

After my father died, we lived in three tiny rooms behind my mother's dress shop. Our kitchen was tiny, almost doll-sized. And yet it was in that little room that Mama taught me how to be at home in the kitchen—to prepare meals for myself and the people I love. I remember so many times when Mama welcomed me home with a baked potato, hot cocoa, cinnamon apples, or popovers in the winter; Popsicles or ice-cold lemonade in the summer.

All these were expressions of love, and they all came from the kitchen.

When our two children were in high school, we lived in a small condominium with a minuscule galley kitchen, and yet we had some wonderful times in that kitchen. We entertained. We worked together. One evening we even served Mexican Mountains (tostadas) to 50 football players and 10 cheerleaders! Jenny and Brad still remember the fun of preparing for that evening—grating cheese, chopping tomatoes, mashing avocados, and slicing olives—and their friends still talk about the fun of crowding into that little condo and overflowing into the garage.

The key to making the best of any kitchen space—spacious or tiny—is to make efficient use of the space you have. But even more important, I believe, is making it a place you love to be.

After all, a large chunk of the average person's lifetime is spent in food-related activities, and many of those take place in the kitchen. If you are a woman 43 years or older, you've already spent more than 50,000 hours in the kitchen. If you're going to make yourself at home, it is only sensible that you will design your kitchen to be homey and comfortable and beautiful, no matter what its size.

One of my favorite features of my current kitchen is the big window with its deep sill. I love to stand by the sink and gaze out toward our pond and our trees, or wave at Bob as he rounds the corner from the garden. And I love the flock of ceramic chickens that peck on my windowsill, the special blue-and-white china that clusters on a little corner shelf, and especially the gathering of family photos that nearly hide my refrigerator door.

Many of my kitchen friends have memories attached: my father's ladle and knife; the shallow, square wooden bowl Bob found at a flea market; the olive-oil canister I have used for many years; the tiny, exquisite cream and sugar set that was an unexpected gift from new acquaintances. At the far end of the room, a "love wall" is crowded with pictures and plaques that were given or created by people we know—even a painting or two by a high school friend of Jenny's.

It doesn't take a major remodeling job to make your kitchen a room you enjoy and feel good in. A fresh paint job, new knobs on the cabinet doors, or just a thorough cleaning and rearranging will do wonders. What about a radio on the shelf, or even a tiny TV? Don't forget a kitchen stool to save your back and legs and a step stool to help you reach those high shelves.

It's also essential to make the kitchen a room in which you can work efficiently. Just a little bit of planning can save countless steps and, over the years, many hours of your time.

The simple rule we've always followed

in our kitchen is "Things that work together go together." Thus, coffeemaker, coffee, sugar bowl and sweetener, and coffee mugs gather together in one cupboard and counter area. Dish towels live next to the sink, pot holders nestle close to the stove, and wooden spoons and spatulas sprout from their holder next to the stove like a cheerful bouquet, cheerfully inviting me and my friends to "come in and use me."

Company in the Kitchen

I have never subscribed to the "keep out of my kitchen" mentality. I love it when my family and guests join me in the kitchen so that we can spend time together while meals are being cooked or special treats are being created.

It's almost second nature to me now.

When guests come, they're part of the family, and that means they're with me in the kitchen.

Sometimes they sit and talk while I get dinner underway.

More often, though, I'll put each person to work, and we'll all have fun together.

First, I'll set out a little plate of hors d'oeuvres that I've prepared for all of us to munch on while dinner's being prepared—something simple, like low-fat tortilla chips and salsa, or some fresh vegetables and dip.

Then, perhaps, I'll pull out our big wooden salad bowl and a few cloves of garlic, and I'll set one guest to mashing the garlic into a paste with salt and pepper, then adding olive oil and vinegar and lemon to make my father's special salad dressing. The greens are torn and laid in the bowl on top of the salad dressing. Then come the tomatoes and the onions and the avocado and the green pepper—whatever luscious ingredients are on hand at the time—and the salad is ready to toss.

This especially is the guest's job. I tell him or her, just as my daddy told me, "Toss it until you think it's all mixed. Then toss it some more." My father always insisted that the tossing was the secret of a good salad. So I was amused and validated to find this Spanish proverb: "Let the salad-maker be a spendthrift for oil, a miser for vinegar, a statesman for salt, and a madman for mixing." Now I guess I'll encourage my company in the kitchen to go just a little mad!

And in the midst of it all, of course, there is talk.

I've had some of my best conversations while I was stirring a pot of soup and someone else was tossing and tossing and tossing that salad. I've had some of my closest times with Bob together in that warm, creative room.

Good talk just seems to happen naturally in the kitchen, whetted by the repetitive work and the wonderful aromas.

Confidences flow easily in that warm, intimate environment.

Creativity flourishes as people work together.

Teamwork clicks into place as one person puts ice in the glasses and another person pulls the napkins into rings and still another one lights the candles.

No one is lonely. No one feels left out— not even the cook.

And then we can all sit down together with a sense of joy and satisfaction. Perhaps, when the meal is over, we will also spend time together as the kitchen is quickly cleaned and readied for the next meal.

This very desire to include everybody in the life of a kitchen has prompted much of the remodeling work we have done in this kitchen.

In fact, one of our first projects in this house was to tear out the wall that separated the kitchen from the great room and put in an open breakfast bar with four high stools. There Bob can sit and do his work while I chop vegetables, or a visitor can sit and talk

while I prepare lunch, or our housekeeper's tiny granddaughter can sit and color while her grandmother takes care of the cleaning chores. Sometimes I'll even throw a quilt over the burners of the range and serve hors d'oeuvres on that bar.

Another major project we undertook to make our kitchen more guest-friendly was the organization of our pantry and cabinets. Quite a few years ago I made the investment of equipping our pantry with matching labeled storage containers. I also replaced the solid cabinet doors with glass ones, and I hung my pots and pans from a rack over the stove. Now it's much easier for someone to come into our kitchen and help me because the guest can find everything at a glance.

I try to put a little thought into making the insides of my cabinets welcoming and attractive. This is not frivolous—I find that it improves my mood and also invites visitors to help out. And it's not difficult—just a matter of lace edging glue-gunned or stapled to the edges of the shelves or a friendly bow tied around one or two items in a cabinet. I even try to keep the refrigerator organized and pretty. I use see-through containers for colorful fruit and vegetables, neatly stacked storage containers for other kinds of food. Sometimes I'll even tuck in a little bouquet of flowers or herbs, just for a cheerful surprise.

And although I generally try to keep my kitchen equipment pared down to what I use often—who wants to spend the time and effort storing and cleaning appliances you never use?—I also invest in duplicates of the items I use often. I keep extra spoons, spatulas, and ladles on hand just so that several people can work at once in my kitchen. I make sure that pot holders are easy to find, that dishcloths are a simple reach away.

I've found that keeping a supply of aprons really helps get everybody into a festive kitchen mood. A pretty apron does so much more than protect your clothes in the kitchen; it also makes people feel like real chefs.

I even keep on hand some chef's hats I bought years ago at a restaurant supply store. The grandchildren love to wear these when they're in the kitchen. And they're in the kitchen a lot, because shared kitchen times are basic to our lives together.

Children at Home in the Kitchen

Kitchens are wonderful and irresistible places for children, and ours were in the kitchen from the time they were tiny. I always tried to have some kind of delicious aroma coming from the oven when my children came home from school—just as my mama did for me. And both children have turned out to be wonderful cooks.

Now our grandchildren are my special kitchen friends. Granddaughter Christine and I have been baking cookies together since she was very tiny, and now she is self-assured as she rolls out buttery scones for our tea parties. She also loves to play waitress and take orders: "I'm here to take your drink orders. We have plain water, ice water, and water with lemon. . . ."

Chad is our scrambled-egg chef and is adept at frying bacon and sausage as well. Bevan, who for years has been Chad's assistant, is moving into his own as a cook. And in the past few years the littlest boys have begun to move into the kitchen, too.

At a recent outdoor family party, for instance, we recruited three-year-old Bradley Joe as a server. Enchanted by the responsibility, he carefully carried out plates and bowls and utensils. Then he carried out mustard and catsup and mayonnaise and carefully placed them on the table. And then came the soy sauce, the Worcestershire sauce, jars of capers and jalapeños, and cartons of butter, milk, and eggs. He became so excited over his kitchen responsibilities that he was emptying the refrigerator!

We thanked him profusely, of course, and told him that we had everything we needed. We were all pleased that at such a young age he was already catching the spirit of the kitchen.

Children need to be in the kitchen not only because it's a center of family warmth, but also because they need to learn kitchen skills. They need to learn to measure and stir and read recipes and plan meals. And they learn so much more at the same time: organization, teamwork, nutrition, even science. (A home-baked loaf of yeast bread is not only a fragrant expression of love; it's also a wonderful lesson in both biology and chemistry: the action of microorganisms, the expansion of gases, the effects of heat on matter, and so much more!)

Yes, having children in the kitchen can be messy. But children are washable, and so is my kitchen. And I consider the extra cleanup time to be a worthwhile investment in a future of happy kitchen hours for myself and this next generation.

I can't wait until the day when I go to visit those children and they invite me into their grown-up kitchens.

Just give me an apron and a chef's hat and hand me the salad bowl.

I'll make like a madman and toss them a salad they won't believe!

I'll toss and I'll toss and I'll toss.

Housewarmings

- Light a candle in your kitchen! Place in on a windowsill or behind the sink to help you see your kitchen duties in a whole new light.

- My friend Carol Lawrence, a wonderful performer who was the original Maria in the musical *West Side Story*, is also a master of the kitchen—and she loves to include her guests in the process. Take a tip from her. Have luscious hors d'oeuvres waiting when guests arrive, then hand each guest an apron and a set of instructions. Carol choreographs her dinners as carefully as her dance numbers— and they work!

- Let your kitchen decor change with the seasons: delicate, new fruits and flowers in spring, a colorful bounty of produce in summer, golden-colored pumpkins and chrysanthemums in fall, and Christmas reds and greens in winter.

- Little lamps in your kitchen are a nice way of adding warm points of light. Try tucking a tiny lamp in a high cabinet with glass doors to showcase some pretty mugs or serving pieces.

- Pretty cotton dish towels make beautiful napkins, placemats, or even café curtains. Or try sewing several together and hanging them across the top of your window to form a cheerful valance.

- If you have the room, why not put a comfy "sitting chair"—a rocking chair or an upholstered chair with footstool—in your kitchen. You'll have more company while you work, and you'll love that chair when your feet give out.

- Store foods in ways that allow them to be decorative as well as useful. Display fruit in a basket or special bowl on the kitchen table or drainboard. Stack potatoes and onions in a basket to enliven an out-of-the-way corner of your counter or floor.

- Next time you make buttered toast, sprinkle on some cinnamon and sugar. An old idea, but when was the last time you did it?

- Keep your olive oil and wine vinegar in pretty decanters by your cooktop. I like to make a seasoned olive oil by combining two dried red peppers (the long, thin kind), the seeds from two more red peppers, one tablespoon each of rosemary and thyme, and four cloves of garlic in a quart jar and covering with olive oil. Or just put a few cloves of garlic in a glass bottle and fill with oil.

- On a slow afternoon, put on soft music and browse through your favorite recipe book for ideas and inspiration.

- Set aside a Saturday morning to learn how to *really* use one of those appliances stored away in a low cabinet. Are you secretly afraid of your pressure cooker? Have you never cooked anything but frozen dinners in your microwave? Has your food processor gathered dust since you bought it? Take the time to find out what these helpers can do, and then decide whether you really require their services. You may be surprised by what goes and what stays.

- Try to keep your kitchen counters free of clutter. The room will look more spacious, and you'll be more inspired to spend time there.

For whom he means to make an often guest,
One dish shall serve; and welcome make the rest.

—JOSEPH HALL

Merry Occasions & Movable Feasts

MAKING MEMORIES WITH SPECIAL CELEBRATIONS

Why have a meal, I've always thought, when you can invest just a little bit more and have a celebration?

I don't mean more money.

I mean a little more thought, a little more caring. Sometimes a little more time or energy. Always, a little more sharing and appreciation.

For that's really what a celebration is.

A sharing. An appreciation. A conscious commitment to joy.

And it takes very little to make that kind of celebration a part of our everyday lives.

Because eating is such a basic part of our existence, the place we eat is the ideal place to celebrate. That should mean the

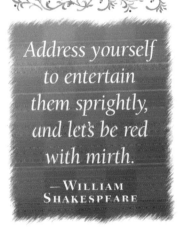

Address yourself to entertain them sprightly, and let's be red with mirth.

—WILLIAM SHAKESPEARE

dining room, of course. I love our dining room, with its aged-brick flooring, its ceiling hung with baskets and dried herbs, its pretty table overlooking the fountain in the courtyard. I love our old icebox (which houses glassware) and the gleaming antique scale above it. I love the treasury of beautiful china and crystal left me by a favorite auntie.

But I have to admit that we don't eat in our dining room very often.

In our home, mealtime celebrations are a movable feast.

My motto is "Have card table, will travel."

Bob and I have celebrated mealtimes in the great room, or the garden room in front of the fire, out by the pond, occasionally in the dining room, often in the breakfast room or perched by the bar in the kitchen, and as often as we can out on the patio or the veranda. We have set up "love feasts" in our bedroom or on the little patio outside it, enjoying special romantic times just for the two of us. We have also set up tables on the lawn to entertain big gatherings of friends and family.

Our meals some- times travel in "love baskets," packed with beautiful china, candles, and flowers. Sometimes they travel on trays. Sometimes we just set up a table somewhere and every- body carries something to it.

At least four times a year, however— often on holidays—we gather around a sparkling, beautifully set dining table, clasp hands to ask a blessing, and sit down together over a special mealtime celebration, rejoicing in the blessings of family and friends and food.

"Eating," writes Alexandria Stoddard, "is the ritual of communion." That's exactly what mealtimes are to Bob and me. They are the times dur- ing the day when we sit down together and share our lives—some- times just with the two of us, sometimes with our family, some- times with treasured friends—nourishing our spirits and our relationships as well as our bodies.

In a sense, it's the time when we are most at home to ourselves and to anyone who is sharing our lives at the moment.

Everyday Warmth

Because I believe mealtimes are so important, I like to make even everyday meals a small celebration.

Our traveling feasts, wherever they take place, are served on pretty dishes (or cheer- ful paper plates) with cloth napkins.

Whenever possible, I like to add a candle or a spray of ivy or a whimsical napkin ring— just a little something to remind us that even everyday eating is a special time of the day.

It goes without saying that we turn off

the television for mealtime—and it's a good idea to let the answering machine take care of the phone. We also try to avoid bringing our arguments and problems to the table. Mealtime is a time for sharing, but also for peace—a moment in the day when we celebrate togetherness and the gift of nourishment.

Yes, I understand that this kind of special touch is not always easy.

If you live alone, setting a pretty table and lighting a candle for an everyday meal can seem like too much trouble, and turning off the television can feel like cutting off your only chance for company.

If you have a busy, active family, just getting everybody to eat at the same time can be difficult enough, and managing to corral everybody into a peaceful meal can seem downright impossible.

It's worth the effort, though, for at least one meal a day.

It's worth making the rules, taking the time, preparing the food—even if it's as simple as macaroni and cheese or take-out pizza. It's worth turning off the noise and turning on the soft music and lighting the candles to make the meal feel warmer and more peaceful. It's worth making the effort to talk and share about the day.

No, it's not easy in this fast-food age to think of everyday meals as celebrations. But every effort you make to think that way is a step toward making yourself and your family more beautifully at home.

Planning for Spontaneous Fun

There will always be times, of course, when you will want to turn the celebration level up a notch, transforming your ordinary mealtimes—or anytime—into special occasions.

I treasure the memories from times of spontaneous merrymaking, when we decided on the spur of the moment to have a party. But these were almost always more successful with a bit of advance planning.

Sound like a contradiction of terms?

It's not. It takes a certain amount of thinking ahead to make spontaneity possible, or at least to widen your possibilities for spontaneous at-home celebrations.

If you have plants and flowers around—either real or silk—you will always have something ready for a centerpiece.

If you stock your freezer with frozen casseroles, you'll always have the wherewithal for a spontaneous feast.

If you maintain your home on a regular

schedule, it will always look ready for a celebration.

So think ahead just a little bit and set up your life to be ready for a party. When party supplies go on sale at the drugstore, I like to stock up on colored plates and napkins, streamers, little gifts, even party hats and noisemakers. When candles are inexpensive, I buy them in bulk and store them in my freezer (to keep them burning longer and cleaner). I keep a roll of cookie dough in my freezer and some scone mix in the pantry and some wonderful, aromatic coffee or tea on my shelves.

And I always keep the teapot clean and shiny, because I never know when the opportunity for a tea party will present itself.

Having a tea party is one of my favorite things to do—a spontaneous celebration that always warms my heart. Because I was once a little girl who had never had a tea party, I never tire of throwing one for the people I love—and it doesn't take much of an occasion to get me going.

Perhaps it will be a good report card. Or an old friend who calls to say he's in town just for the evening. Or a project that is finished, a crisis that is over. Or I simply realize it's been too long since our last party.

Whatever the reason, I'm ready.

Out of the cabinet comes my pretty lace tablecloth.

Out of the armoire come the teacups of our choice.

A flick of the match brings me candlelight.

Within minutes the teakettle is whistling, cookies have appeared from the freezer, and the smell of delicious cinnamon tea is drifting through the house.

It all takes just minutes, and it can make my day.

I might even throw a little confetti on the table—just for the fun of celebrating.

"Big-Deal" Celebrations

This doesn't mean, of course, that all your at-home celebrations will be spur-of-the-moment. Sometimes it is really fun to throw an "event," complete with written invitations, elaborate decorations, and lavish foods. And even a very formal dinner can be gracious and fulfilling, deeply satisfying and filled with the spirit of celebration. Your meticulous planning and loving preparation, your most beautiful tablecloths and place settings and centerpieces—all can be wonderful ways to tell your guests that you care enough to plan for their visit.

A birthday, a holiday, a family reunion—all these can be reasons to pull out the stops and have a party. A "big-deal" celebration can be informal: a barbecue, a pizza party, or even a covered-dish get-together. Or it can be beautifully formal, complete with linen cloth and sparkling crystal.

For me in the last few years, these are the times when I bring out my auntie's beautiful china and crystal, my crisp, white linen tablecloths, my crystal candle holders. These are the times when Jenny helps me arrange beautiful flowers for a centerpiece, when I plan for days in advance, when I write place cards and plan little gifts for each guest. We don't do this very often in our home—we really live quite informally—but we treasure these times of special celebration in our lives.

Don't let the prospect of such a celebration daunt you.

It's not only doable, it's delightful.

Remember, a festive occasion doesn't need to be stiff. And it doesn't even have to be expensive. It's simply a matter of using the best that you have and investing your best with the spirit of celebration.

I never owned a set of good china until my auntie passed away just a few years ago. In the early years of our marriage, we owned very little at all. But that never stopped us from planning big, beautiful dinner parties. We would put out the best that we had. Sometimes we would borrow platters and serving pieces. Occasionally we even rented table linens or silver. We used our imagination. We made liberal use of candlelight magic—even the plainest pieces can look beautiful when candles are lit.

There is no law that says everything on your table has to match, all of your dishes must have a fancy name on the bottom, your special planned parties must be stiff and formal.

The only real requirements are beauty and warmth and a little bit of extra effort—taking the time to plan something that is better than ordinary.

One of the very special occasions in our home for more than a decade has been granddaughter Christine's annual birthday tea party. We started this tradition when she was quite tiny. We would bake cookies and make tea together, set a pretty table, dress up, and then enjoy our tea.

Later, as Christine grew, her parties grew, too. We began the tradition of inviting a friend to share her special party, and the two of them took more and more responsibility for planning and preparing. A beautiful tea table would be set in the tree house or out by the pond or up in the loft, and Christine and her friend would have a wonderful time sipping tea and chatting like grown-up ladies.

This year, however, when Christine turned 13, we made plans for a special high tea for several of her friends. Everyone came dressed in her Sunday best. We escorted the girls out on our veranda, where we had laid out a silver tea service on a white linen cloth. And then I brought out a tray of dainty demitasse teacups, antique embroidered hankies, and tiny silver spoons—the product of a months-long search through antique shops. Although not expensive, each cup was different and lovely. I let each girl pick a cup, a hankie to use as a napkin (serviette), and a spoon.

We had a lovely tea, with Christine's special scones, jam, and real whipped cream. We collected all the cups and spoons, washed and dried them, and handed them back to the girls. Then I told them all a story.

"The teacup you hold in your hand," I said, "is beautiful. And you are beautiful, too, handmade by God. But look at your teacup. Do you see a chip or crack? As you grow older, certain things may happen that can hurt or even damage you. Maybe a boyfriend will jilt you or a college won't accept you. Those little cracks and chips come into everyone's life. But look at your teacup; it's still beautiful, and it can still be used. And you can stay beautiful and useful, too, if you keep growing and learning."

They were all listening, intent on what I was saying, studying their cups. When I got through, one of those girls practically screamed, "Oh, I'm so excited; my cup has a chip in it."

And then I told them, "The teacup you are holding in your hands is yours to keep." They were thrilled. Each girl carefully toted home a china demitasse, a hankie, and a little silver spoon. I hope that years later, and especially during times of sadness, they'll remember the special day that was Christine's thirteenth birthday.

I know I certainly will.

Even When Something Goes Wrong

Special celebrations, you see, are the stuff that memories are made of. They are worth the effort you put into them, worth the money you spend (although it doesn't have to be a fortune), worth the planning and the painstaking preparations.

And yet your special celebrations don't have to be perfect in order to be wonderful and memorable. Sometimes your plans will go awry. Sometimes problems will crop up. Sometimes everything will seem to conspire to ruin your wonderful at-home celebration.

In my experience, even these near-disasters can lead the way to even more memorable and more wonderful celebrations. The key is to remain flexible and to be ready to try plan B. Often you'll find that plan B was the celebration you really wanted in the first place.

That happened to me this Thanksgiving. The day before the holiday, I would have been panicked if I hadn't been so depressed.

A flu bug the week before had left me a little wobbly to start with. A holiday seminar over the weekend had kept me away from home until Tuesday night, physically drained, wondering where I was going to summon the energy to prepare Thanksgiving for 20 people: our children and their fami-

lies, a cousin and his family, and a few friends.

When I walked into the house on Tuesday evening, I felt a surge of hope and encouragement. Our daughter, Jenny, had come over while we were away and completely set the table with a beautiful centerpiece and my auntie's sparkling china and crystal. The dining room was a vision, the house was spotless and shining; all that was left for me to do was cook.

But we weren't through with our disasters yet. That was the afternoon the roofers came over to do some repair work. And not only did their banging sift dirt and dust down on that beautiful Thanksgiving table, but it also dislodged one of the many baskets that hang from the ceiling of our dining room, shattering two of my auntie's irreplaceable crystal goblets from Europe. At that point I was near tears. I would have to start all over again.

My friend Sally, who was helping me clean, gently cleared off all those dishes, washed and dried the ones that were intact, and swept away the shattered crystal. With a bit of dusting, Jenny's centerpiece was ready to put back on the table, and the table was reset.

Then I sat down to do my annual Thanksgiving "I love you because..." cards.

For many years this has been a Thanksgiving tradition with me. It's one way for me to give thanks for the people I love. So I write out little cards that say, "I love you because...you always have a cheerful smile" or "I love you because...you have a willing spirit" or "I love you because...you can always make me laugh."

This year, as I sat down to write, I didn't feel thankful; I felt overwhelmed. I was grateful to Jenny and to Sally, but I still had that feeling that the whole holiday was my responsibility and that I just wasn't up to it this time. Yes, people always offered to help, but even the task of delegating chores seemed like too much work.

And then it came to me. I realized that all the people who loved me were sincere in their desire to help; all they needed was a sense of where they were needed. So I picked up the first "I love you because..." card and wrote, "I love you because...you get to serve the dessert."

The next card read, "I love you because . . . you get to wash the dishes" and the next one announced, "I love you because . . . you

get to mash the potatoes."

I wrote enough cards for everyone who was coming, folded each one in half, and placed them all in a basket. I was still a little nervous. *Will they think I'm taking advantage of them?* But as my family and friends arrived that day, I let each of them draw from the "I love you" basket—and they were thrilled! Each adult and every child attended to his or her duties seriously but cheerfully, and the day breezed by happily.

This Thanksgiving turned out to be a wonderful celebration for all of us. The children loved playing with little games I had put on the table before the meal began. After dessert, we each lit a candle by our neighbor's plate and told why that person was special. We talked. We laughed a lot. We cried a little.

And later, as we went around the table and each shared what we were thankful for, I could say with grateful sincerity, "I am thankful for family and friends who care enough to gather with me and to help me make celebrating a wonderful part of our at-home living."

Housewarmings

- Make celebration a tradition in your family. Celebrate everything: good days, bad days that are finally over, birthdays, nonbirthdays.

- Little touches can make a big difference in making your meals into celebrations. Instead of just plopping the containers on the table, try putting your whipped butter in a white pottery crock or serving catsup in a pretty bowl with a spoon.

- Have fun with theme parties when you entertain. One of our all-time favorite parties was a "piggy party" where everyone came in pink. We ate "greens and hog rinds" (spinach salad with bacon), "sausage slop" (stew), and "mud pie" for dessert.

- You can make wonderful, colorful table linens—tablecloths, napkins, runners—out of sheets. But you'll never regret investing in a beautiful white-linen tablecloth. Properly cared for, it will last you a lifetime.

- Get your children involved preparing for a dinner party. They can make place cards, set the table, help you cook, create the centerpiece. Our children were always assigned to greet guests at the door and take their coats—a wonderful opportunity for teaching hospitality and manners.

- For a festive touch at the table, "gift-wrap" the place settings with wide ribbon or strips of gauze. Stack plate, salad plate, bowl, and glass on top of two crossed ribbons. Gently bring ribbons up around the place setting and tie in a big, floppy bow, or add a pre-tied bow. Tie scraps of the same ribbon around napkins as napkin rings.

- Birthday or not, everyone loves a present. Often I place a tiny gift by our dinner guests' plates: a book, a pen, an antique hankie, or a pot holder tied with a bow.

- Let your sharing extend beyond your family and friends. Several times a year create a "love basket" filled with food for a needy family. Or try spending part of your holidays helping out at a local rescue mission.

- Celebrate your family's cultural heritage—Italian, Scottish, Mexican, Chinese, or American heartland—with a special kind of dinner party. Or celebrate somebody else's heritage, perhaps a friend or neighbor's. If the food and customs are unfamiliar to you, buy a book or ask someone to teach you. Play appropriate music, eat native food, even learn a folk dance!

- If you have the right attitude, even mishaps and mistakes can become fun traditions in your family. One family I know turned a birthday-cake disaster—one layer sliding off the other—into an occasion for laughter. They just frosted the cake as it was and enjoyed it. After that, something *always* had to be wrong with the cake—a perfect cake would have been a disappointment.

- Just once during the summer, turn dinner into celebration time by serving sundaes or banana splits for your main meal. It's a lot less fattening than dinner *plus* banana splits, and the one time won't ruin anyone's health.

- Thank-you notes are traditional after you've taken part in a celebration in someone's home, but you can thank your guests as well. The next time you have company, surprise them by writing a thank-you as soon as they leave, thanking them for sharing your event and your life.

*A home needs not only candles and confetti to make it joyful—
a home also needs connection. Candles offer the spirit of
warmth. Confetti adds the spirit of celebration. And connections
tie warmth and celebration together with love.*

—LINDSEY O'CONNOR

Intimate Spaces

THE REST AND ROMANCE OF BED AND BATH

You can see it in your dreams— this beautiful, restful, romantic place that is all your own.

This is the blissful bower where you take your weary body for a rejuvenating cat-nap, a peaceful night of slumber, or a restful moment with a favorite book. It's a cozy, intimate chamber where you enjoy special moments with the people who are closest to you—including your very own self! It's a pampering retreat where you let yourself be refreshed and renewed and readied to start again.

Your bedroom and bathroom are the intimate spaces of your home, the places where you can go and shut the door and be most deeply you. They are your private chambers, the settings for your most intimate activities. Shouldn't they be the most

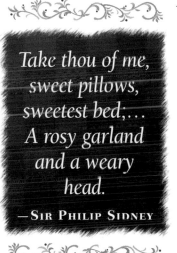

Take thou of me, sweet pillows, sweetest bed;… A rosy garland and a weary head.

—SIR PHILIP SIDNEY

beautiful, the most welcoming, the most inviting rooms in your house?

Unfortunately, though, they are often just the opposite.

As a society, we are impatient with the idea of rest. We are uncomfortable with closeness and intimacy. For all our talk about "taking care of ourselves," we tend to focus on our outer lives and neglect our inner ones. And I think this fact is reflected in many of the bedrooms and baths I see (or hear about, because women are embarrassed to take me into their private rooms).

All too often, these rooms are the afterthoughts of the house. They are the last to be decorated, the first to fill up with clutter.

The master bedroom becomes the place where the clothes baskets and the mail pile up. This is the room where unsightly junk is thrown behind closed doors when unexpected guests arrive. Dressers are piled high, the television blares, and toys clutter the floor. Sometimes there is a crib, a playpen, an ironing board or a baby swing. The bathroom, too, especially a private bathroom, becomes a place where hand-washables dangle or magazines pile up in a corner.

And all this is understandable. When time is short, it's tempting to concentrate on the areas people see and let the other areas go. But these are the very rooms where you need to make yourself most beautifully at home. You should feel comfortable and welcome and rested in these rooms, for they are the starting places for a generous and welcoming spirit.

Most of us spend an average of ten hours a day in our bedrooms and baths—dressing, undressing, exercising, reading, reflecting, sewing, writing, puttering, talking on the phone or watching television, playing with children, sleeping, eating, putting on makeup, and so on. At this rate we could and will spend half our lives in our bedrooms—and we spend one-third of our lives actually in bed!

If at all possible, therefore, these rooms should be your most beautiful private sanctuary. They should be the first rooms you decorate, making them all you wish them to be. They should be serene and beautiful—rooms that invite you to peaceful, intimate sharing.

A Place to Retreat

It helps to think of your bedroom as your own personal retreat center—a place where quiet beauty wraps itself around you and slumber beckons, a place where you can kick off your shoes and shed the stress of the day.

Ask yourself what kind of atmosphere you want to create. A garden of soft pastels and greens? Bright colors that give you energy? Perhaps an earthy collage of rusts, golds, and browns, or a seascape of clear blue and sunny pastels? Whatever the colors and the decorations, make this the happiest and most restful room in your world.

Let your five senses lead you, and include whatever quiets and relaxes you. Consider the feel of the sheets—cool cotton or cozy flannel. Scent the air with potpourri or candles or even incense. Toss a woolly afghan over the end of the bed or on a chair to wrap around you for a nap. A good lamp by the bedside invites you to read in bed. A radio or tape recorder nearby lifts your spirits with beautiful music or keeps you company with quiet talk.

To create a welcoming retreat, surround yourself with what you love. Everything that you find comforting and soothing should welcome you into your private chambers. Every surface should seem to smile.

That's the way I feel when I walk into our sunny bedroom or even see it through the open French doors as I walk by. Our big, soft Rice bed with its beautifully carved posts calls out to me, beckoning me to climb up and have a rest.

I love the bed coverings a cheerful yellow comforter in summer, the pastel patchwork in winter, with always a snuggly extra throw for naps. I love the piles of puffy pillows, the Victorian art prints topped with garlands of silk flowers. I love the ceiling fan that turns lazily overhead, stirring the breeze, and the glowing lamps that light my rest-time reading. I love the subtly patterned area rug that softens the hardwood floor.

This room is sunny but private, with French doors opening onto a tiny enclosed patio, with a big bay window that embraces a long, low chest, with my comfy wing-backed chair and a flock of family photos that remind me always of who I am and of those I love. Even the things I can't see—the clothes and jewelry and keepsakes tucked away in the closet and the armoire and the ancient humpbacked trunk—add to the feeling of serene comfort.

The furniture in this room was not bought as a set. One bedside table is an antique coal bin; the other, an old oak table covered with a cross-stitched cloth. The chest of drawers that fills the bay window is a remnant from a set we had years ago. The wing chair belonged to my mother. The golden oak armoire gleams with a different patina than the dark bed and the barnwood walls. The white Battenberg lace dust ruffle echoes the Battenberg cloth on a round table nearby and the clean, white beauty of the window and door frames.

And yet, somehow it all comes together. It all shares the same spirit of beauty and rest and romance.

In past years I have slept in many different rooms—in hotels and homes and wonderful bed-and-breakfast places. But I never rest quite as well as when I am here in my very own restful retreat center.

I am never quite so at-home as when I am in my very own beautiful bed.

A Setting for Romance

But it's not just my bedroom, of course.

I share this room with my Bob, the love of my life, my partner in work and play and romance. And we both value our bedroom as the site of our most intimate sharing.

When we come in here, the door closes behind us.

No matter who is in the rest of the house, here it's just the two of us, and here is where we nurture the inner life of our marriage.

We spend hours talking and dreaming—building our closeness by sharing our hearts. We make love here. We read to each other from the books by our bedside. Sometimes we bring in a tray and enjoy a cup of tea or a cozy breakfast in bed, or we set up the card table and enjoy a leisurely romantic dinner. Dinner comes in a basket from the kitchen—perhaps a simple pasta dish, a salad, and a mouthwatering dessert. Then we just sit and eat and enjoy the romance of being together, just the two of us.

For this truly is a romantic room—a place not only of love, but of sensual delight, of delicious textures and beautiful sights and sensuous aromas and wonderful tastes. We work to keep it that way, paying special attention to the soft lighting, to the smoothness of the sheets, to the freshness of the flowers. I love to put a bouquet of fresh flowers next to Bob's side of the bed!

We also work to keep ourselves attractive to the other—through our grooming, through the clothes we wear, and also in the way we treat each other. We try to keep our conversations uplifting, not putting each other down. We make time for one another, concocting romantic surprises, sharing activities, or just being together. We make it a priority to be sensitive to each other.

Often, of course, our romantic life will be a movable feast: a blanket under the stars, a weekend at a wonderful bed and breakfast, a walk around the block. Our relationship thrives in our work and in our family as well as in our bedroom.

But so much of it happens right here, in these private rooms we share. This is the headquarters for the adventure of our love and our lives together. I try to keep it beautiful and intimate, to set a lovely stage for the drama of our shared times.

Bob and I have had many happy times in our room, and some difficult, heart-hurting times as well. But the memories always bring smiles when we've shared the true spirit of refuge and romance in our own private space.

A Place to Be Close

Our husband-and-wife times are not the only kinds of intimate sharing that take place in this room, of course.

This is also a place where I share special closeness with other people I love.

When our children were small, for instance, they would come to our bed to snuggle and be close on a lazy vacation morning, or when a thunderstorm or earthquake left them frightened.

Now, years later, this is the place where the grandchildren will crawl up with me to listen to a story. Sometimes we'll just snuggle together and talk, and I'll rub their feet. Sometimes we'll stretch out and share a nap time with a blankie or a floppy stuffed animal.

These private rooms have also proved to be a wonderful place for sharing with dear friends. Here the spirit of the slumber party can reign, with shared confidences, shared laughter, and perhaps a beauty secret or two.

One of my favorite bedroom memories is of an afternoon when my friend Barbara DeLorenzo came over for a visit. We both climbed up on my bed with a cup of tea and talked and relaxed together while the afternoon sun streamed in through the French doors. I cherish the memory of that wonderful, lazy afternoon—a time of sharing with a dear friend.

The intimate sharing that our bedroom invites, by the way, is the primary reason we have chosen to banish the television from this room. To me, turning on a television is like bringing the outside world into my home. It demands my attention in a way that a stereo or a book will not do.

In my bedroom and bath, I simply don't want that intrusion. I want to reserve this space to share with the ones who are closest to me: my Bob, my children and grandchildren, a few special friends. And myself as well . . . for my bedroom is one of my most important sources of healing solitude.

The renewing influence of solitude is more precious than ever today, when noise and clamor seem to close in on us from all sides. Most of us work, play, and go to school to a constant background of traffic and TV. We fight crowds at the mall, in restaurants, and on the highway. Life seems more competitive and stressful than ever before. To people who are overstimulated and worn down by the constant barrage of modern living, the stillness of a private space can be a literal lifesaver.

My bedroom is one of the places I go to find that stillness. Here I can shut the door and find space to be quiet, to read and think and dream. Sometimes I will write in my journal, letting my thoughts grow clearer as they distill on the page. Often I will meditate or pray, letting my spirit be guided and renewed. Sometimes I will simply lie still and breathe deeply and thankfully, enjoying the stillness and the comfort.

We all need a place for private, intimate aloneness—a place where we can be at home in the stillness and come to know ourselves for who we really are. If our private rooms are lovely and romantic and inviting, our inner lives will be nourished, and our outer lives cannot help but be better.

A Place for Restoration

I think of our big master bathroom as an extension of our bedroom space. It, too, is private and beautiful and restful and romantic. And it, too, is a place for both sharing and solitude.

That is one reason for the big iron bathtub—it easily holds two adults for a bubble bath and a talk, or several babies for a rubber-ducky session. The shower, too, is spacious and sunny, accommodating to two schedules. At the same time, this is my most private space—the place where I take care of myself. If my bedroom is my place of retreat, this is my place for restoration and revitalization.

What is more wonderful and relaxing than a half hour of soaking in a warm tub filled with fragrant bubbles? What is more revitalizing than a tingling shower with a citrus-scented bath gel? What is more uplifting than emerging clean from a bath, drying your hair, and fixing your face? Sometimes, especially if your children are small, your moments in the bathroom may be your only time to yourself!

And all these are reasons to make the bath just as beautiful and inviting as the rest of the house.

That is why we have draped the ivy around the big oak mirror and filled the shelves with plants and beautiful objects as well as shampoo and toothbrushes. That is why we have lined the shelves with lace and filled little bowls with fragrant potpourri.

That is why we stock up on sweet-smelling oils and powders and load the linen closet with big, fluffy towels.

My memories surround me here, too. Some special pieces of my mother's jewelry rest in a few of her little glass jewel boxes. A little floral festoon that Jenny made graces the window. Two or three antique soaps in their original wrappers remind me of the time Bob discovered them in an antique shop. These are all the things that lift my spirit and help me return to the rest of my household with open arms and a welcoming spirit.

And the decor in my bath is not all standard "bathroom issue"—the matching terry mat and toilet cover, the little plastic or ceramic soap and toothbrush holders. I think it's much more charming to decorate this most private of rooms the same way you would decorate your other rooms—to make it lovely and inviting and interesting.

I treasure one of my favorite features of our bathroom because of its uniqueness. We've installed a glassed-in lawyer's case full of little treasures: some teacups, antique hankies, and a few old toys. We believe that little case adds a unique touch, as well as giving us something to look at during long sessions in the tub.

I've seen other wonderful, creative ideas in bathrooms I have visited. One featured a lovely hooked rug instead of a standard bath mat. One bathroom featured family photos (copies, not originals) in antique oval frames. Yet another treated the toilet tank as a little curio shelf, with a cloth drape, photograph, and a pretty plant. Yet another used a lovely china bowl to hold tiny soaps and a pretty basket to hold magazines.

The lighting in your bathroom must, of course, be bright enough for shaving and applying makeup. But I like to tuck some little low-watt lamps in the corners for when the utility lights are turned off. They add not only a soft glow, but also a beautiful decorator touch.

And don't forget the candles!

I like to take a hint from my daughter, Jenny, who used to take all three of her children into the bathroom with her when everyone was getting on everyone else's nerves. There she would light candles, run a foamy bubble bath, and plop all the children in together. She would sit and read or rest in the candlelight while the babies played, and all four would emerge pink-faced and happy, with their clean faces and their good spirits restored.

Dreams Coming True

That, of course, is the ultimate purpose of your private chambers—the places where you rest and relax and refresh yourself.

These are the rooms that extend open arms to you so that you can open your arms to others.

And that is why beauty and comfort in your private space is not a luxury.

Do your private rooms welcome you? Have you expended the same effort for the places where you retreat as you have for the places where you welcome guests?

Are you happy and at home in your most intimate space and your most intimate relationships?

If that is true, you will have a home base for beauty and serenity, a spiritual center for at-homeness.

These rooms will be the place where your at-home dreams come true.

HOUSEWARMINGS

IDEAS FOR BEAUTIFUL PRIVATE ROOMS

- Arrange your bedroom furniture so that the first thing you see as you enter is the bed. Cover it with a beautiful, inviting quilt or spread, pile it with pillows, and rejoice in the sense of welcome.

- A made-up bed is always more welcoming and relaxing than a tangle of sheets. Make a rule in your house that the last one out of the bed makes it up. If you rebel at wrestling with layers of sheets, blankets, and bedspreads, simplify matters with a comforter or a duvet.

- Clutter wearies the spirit and fights against serenity. At the very least, take 15 minutes to dejunk the room where you spend your quiet time.

- Keep a journal and an inspirational book on your bedside table for spiritual food and intimate expression during still moments. Don't forget to have a pen or pencil at hand.

- Sheets are one of your greatest tools for quickly and inexpensively updating the look of your private rooms. I have used sheets to make pillows, wall coverings, comforter covers—and even as sheets!

- For a beautiful, romantic touch, use a glue gun to cover an inexpensive white lampshade with lace, or borrow a tip from the Victorians and drape a pink or red cloth over a lampshade to cast a rosy glow around the room. (To avoid scorching, do this only with low-watt bulbs and natural fabrics.)

- Garland a large picture with a swag of greenery or flowers for a decorator touch. In the winter, silk evergreens look festive.

- The dream pillow is an old and charming way to encourage sweet sleep and sweet dreams. Mix hops (to encourage sleep), lavender (for pleasant dreams), rosemary (for help in recalling dreams), thyme (to prevent nightmares), and rose petals (for dreams of love) and sew into small muslin pillows to tuck inside your pillowcase.

- It's easy to fill your dreams and your dresser drawers with fragrance by creating your own sachets. For a sachet, place a little potpourri in a lace handkerchief and tie with a narrow ribbon. For a beautiful bath sachet, mix fragrant herbs (rose petals, lavender, or rosemary), quick oats, table salt, and essential oils (available from a health-food store). Tie in little muslin bags with twine or waterproof ribbon and hang under running water as the tub fills.

- For wonderful ideas about decorating a bedroom or bath, browse through the bed-and-bath section of a department store or gift shop. Don't be afraid to adapt and copy.

- Don't restrict your restful or romantic touches to the bed and bath—just start there. Everyone in the family can enjoy candles, soft fabrics, touches of lace, and warm, cozy comfort.

My idea of a home is a house in which each member of the family can on the instant kindle a fire in his or her private room.

—RALPH WALDO EMERSON

Fit for a Princess

Once upon a time, there was a beautiful young girl named Jenny who dreamed of being a princess.

She loved to listen to those wonderful stories about princesses of old—especially the one about the princess and the pea. She acted out that story when she played dress-up, and she retold it to her dolls with wonder in her voice.

Once she even tried placing a pea under her own mattress to see if she was a real princess. Apparently she wasn't—yet. But she kept wishing and hoping and dreaming, and eventually her dream did come true. That is, her family, who loved her very much, began calling her Princess Jenny. And the room where she slept and dreamed and made herself at home became known as the Princess Room.

Eventually, of course, Princess Jenny grew up and went off to college. She packed up her bags and left the Princess Room behind—but it wasn't empty long.

That pretty, comfortable room soon became the place where guests stayed when they came to spend the night. They would smile and get a little excited when they were told, "Oh, you get to sleep in the Princess Room."

> *Come in the evening,*
> *or come in the morning,*
> *Come when you're*
> *looked for, or come*
> *without warning,*
> *Kisses and welcome*
> *you'll find here*
> *before you,*
> *And the oftener you*
> *come here the more*
> *I'll adore you.*
>
> —THOMAS O. DAVIS
> (FROM AN IRISH PROVERB)

The Royal Treatment

The princess in this story, of course, is our own daughter, Jenny, and the Princess Room is the name we still use for the bedroom set aside for overnight guests. We've had a Princess Room in four houses. Not only does the royal-sounding name bring amusement to our guests and recall happy memories for us, but it also paints a picture of the way we want everybody to feel when they come to stay with us, whether or not they spend the night.

We want our guests to feel like royalty.

We want every person who visits our home to feel pampered, appreciated, and loved.

And we want this kind of royal hospitality to be built into the fabric of our everyday lives, so that on the spur of any moment we can say, "Please come to our house and spend some time with us."

To us, hospitality is so much more than entertaining, so much more than menus and decorating and putting on a show. Instead, it's a matter of organizing our lives so there's always room for one more—always an extra place at the table or an extra pillow and blanket, always a welcome for those who need a listening ear or a place to stay the night.

You really don't need elaborate preparations to share that kind of hospitality. You certainly don't need a special room just for guests. Hospitality can thrive in the simplest of settings and the humblest of circumstances. It's a matter of opening your life to others, giving them the best you have to offer, but never allowing elaborate preparations to substitute for an open-armed welcome.

Our entire house, in fact, is set up around this principle of hospitality. We love to welcome guests for a meal, an evening, or just a cup of tea. And we love to extend the invitation for people to spend a night or two in our Princess Room. To us, this is sharing our lives on a deeper level. When we go to bed and wake up in the same house with someone, we can't help but know them a little better. We can't help but feel they've somehow become a part of our home, a part of our lives, and that our lives are richer for the time we spent together.

A Room for Royalty

Our current Princess Room has been the focus of all my most feminine, romantic dreams—a real joy to put together. Yellow-striped Laura Ashley wallpaper brightens the walls, and a coordinating border of roses sets the lush, romantic mood. The high, antique oak bed with its comfortable mattress wears an Amish quilt in pastel shades and a pile of puffy white pillows. (I usually have a doll or a stuffed animal playing around the pillows.) A freshly starched lace cloth on the bedside table sets off an oil lamp and family photos, and built-in shelves hold books, mementos, and teacups. An old iron lamp with frosted glass sheds its light on bedtime reading. The old-fashioned rocking chair cuddles a teddy bear in its lap.

Best of all is the window seat with its cozy quilt cover. More pillows fill the seat and invite guests to relax and enjoy the view of trees and pond. The hardwood floor is gentled and warmed by an Oriental area rug that echoes the colors in the room. On the walls hang beautiful Victorian-looking prints of teacups and teapots.

This room has its own bath—a cheerful, yellow-tiled room with a glassed-in shower and fresh white bath mat and towels. In the bathroom drawers I stock a host of travel extras—toothpaste, razors, shampoo, even a hair dryer—and the tile counters hold a fragrant bowl of potpourri and a softly glowing night-light.

This room is not an afterthought to us. It is integral to our goal of building a beautiful life and then sharing it with others. So we have put as much energy and effort into decorating our guest room and making it irresistibly inviting as we have any room in our house.

I have even been known to sneak in here and steal a nap when no one is staying with us. The mattress and the pillows are soft and inviting. The breeze from the windows over the bed is intoxicating—sweet with the smell of orange blossoms or roses from the arbor nearby. Through the big bay window in front you can see the glint of sunlight on our pond, and the big plastic Canada geese, which look amazingly real, seem ready to turn and honk hello.

Hospitable Essentials

We hope we have created a cozy, warm, loving experience for our guests who sleep in the Princess Room.

But—and this is very important—you don't have to have a special room in order to make your overnight guests feel special. (We certainly didn't when our own princess was in residence!) I have stayed in many homes as I travel the country, and I can testify that little touches of caring and welcome can make even the most humble quarters comfortable and hospitable.

After all, the key to successful hospitality is being sensitive to the needs of your guests, and you can do that in any setting, especially with a little bit of advance planning. Both the way you set up your guest quarters and the way your treat your guests when they arrive can make visiting your home a royal experience.

What are the essentials of overnight hospitality?

The most important thing, of course, is a comfortable place to sleep. The ideal is a comfortable bed with a quality mattress and foundation. A quality sofa bed or futon provides a good alternative, especially if you supplement these thinner mattresses with a foam mattress or an "egg crate" mattress pad. (Between visits, these can be rolled up and stored in the back of a closet.) Some of the better-quality air mattresses can also be quite comfortable for short stays. Children and younger guests can be quite happy on a pallet made up of comforters or a sleeping bag on the floor. In fact, the children in your own household might be very happy to give up their beds to guests in return for the adventure of sleeping on the floor.

Remember that comfort is the key to hospitable guest quarters. Be sure you personally try out your guest bed, sofa bed, futon, or cot. If you can't get a good night's sleep there, your guests won't either.

It goes without saying that you should provide fresh linens for an overnight guest. Sheets of fine-grained cotton or even silk in the summer or fuzzy flannel in the winter raise the comfort level a notch. So can embroidered pillowcases and large, plush towels. An extra blanket, a comforter, or a fan can be a godsend if the temperature changes suddenly in the night.

After a comfortable sleeping place, a guest needs privacy—room to dress and think and retreat. If you have a separate guest room, this is easy. If not, a little ingenuity can provide your guests with space. It's a good idea, for example, to set up your guest bed in a room that is not needed on an everyday basis. Perhaps an office or a den could serve as temporary guest quarters, abandoning its usual purpose for the space of a visit. If guests must sleep in a more public area (such as on the sofa), take care to keep the family elsewhere some of the time, giving guests a little while to relax in peace.

It's always a good idea to clear away some of your own things in order to make space for your guest. If possible, empty out a part of a closet and a drawer or two. At the very least, set aside a corner for luggage and provide some hooks for hanging coats and dresses. In the bathroom, a rack or hook for special towels and some counter space for toiletries will be appreciated.

Golden-Rule Hospitality

Once these basics are provided, some imaginative extra touches can make a big difference. These are the little extras that say "I care."

An adequate, well-placed reading light plus an assortment of books and current magazines help guests prepare for sleep. A comfortable chair provides a place to relax or to put on shoes.

A good clock radio provides both music and a sense of independence, while a bowl of fruit or a pitcher of water takes care of midnight munchies.

And beautiful objects—fresh flowers, lovely pictures, scented candles, interesting mementos—help create a welcoming and personal atmosphere.

But royal treatment is not just a matter of how you prepare for guests. It is also a matter of what you do for your guests while they are with you.

If I have time, for instance, I like to sneak into the guest room after dinner and turn down the sheets. (I have even been known to leave a mint.) I refresh the supply of towels in the bath and empty the wastebasket. I leave a copy of a book or magazine I love on the bedside table or a simple gift in a beautifully wrapped package.

And I love to bring my guests a morning tray. This has become almost a trademark of the "Barnes' bed and breakfast." A fragrant cup of coffee or tea or a steaming mug of cocoa served with toast and jelly accompanied by a lit candle is a simple way to make anyone feel special—a wonderful affirmation of the joy of sharing your lives through hospitality.

There are so many hospitable extras that can make your guests' stay a royal experience. You just need a little empathy, a little imagination, a little creativity, plus a willingness to make sharing your life and your home a priority.

Not Just for Company

The royal treatment in your home should not be reserved for guests.

I really believe that treating people like royalty should be an everyday practice extended to those who share our lives as well as those who come to visit.

A few summers ago, while we were on vacation, my Bob injured his knee playing tennis. Several days after we arrived home, the pain became so intense that Bob decided to spend the morning in bed. Here, at last, was an opportunity for me to share hospitality and prepare breakfast in bed for my Bob—something I often do for overnight guests. The tray was splendid with fresh, hot coffee in a pretty china cup and saucer, steaming bran muffins, fruit and coconut, granola, fresh-squeezed orange juice, a vase of freshly picked flowers, and a candle.

Bob's eyes spoke volumes as I fluffed up the pillows and placed the tray on his lap.

"How beautiful!" he exclaimed. "And just for me?" Weeks later, he was still talking about his breakfast in bed.

I realized it was the first time in more than 35 years I had ever wakened my Bob, whom I love so deeply, with a beautiful breakfast tray. Since that occasion I've decided to try giving Bob the royal treatment more often, even when he's perfectly healthy.

I've also tried to treat other family members a bit more royally—myself included.

When the grandchildren are visiting, for instance, it's a simple matter of serving them cookies on a pretty platter or setting their place with a bright-red "You Are Special" plate.

When Brad and Maria come, it's a matter of leaving a little personal gift in their room or letting them enjoy a quiet dinner on the patio while we take care of their children.

And when I'm dining alone, it doesn't take that much more effort to set a pretty table and light a candle than it does to slap the frozen dinner on the table. It's not that much harder to treat myself to a warm bubble bath, a soothing drink, and freshly turned-down sheets instead of just falling into bed.

It really doesn't take much to give anybody the princess treatment, and the payoffs are immense in terms of warm hospitality, enriched friendships, and widened horizons.

It's just one more step toward living happily and comfortably ever after.

Housewarmings

∾ What aspect of your home or apartment do you enjoy most: the view, the quiet, the yard? Let that aspect be the focus of your hospitality. Share the aspects of your life that bring you the most pleasure.

∾ Have a little bit of fun with the idea of giving guests and family the royal treatment. Make a little crown out of gold paper and carry it in along with a breakfast-in-bed tray, or use it to designate a guest of honor at a family meal.

∾ Piles of pillows are a relatively inexpensive way to add a luxuriously hospitable touch to any room. It's a good idea to provide several different kinds of pillows—firm, soft, and at least one hypoallergenic—so that guests can sleep on one that feels familiar. Big, square European pillows are nice for reading in bed.

∾ One of the big hits in our guest bathroom is a big, fluffy terry robe hanging on the back of the bathroom door. If you love that touch in fancy hotels, why not invest in it for your own home?

∾ Save the complimentary bottles of shampoo and lotion, the little sewing kits, and shoeshine cloths you receive in nice hotels (or buy from the "travel-size" rack in a drug-store). Include a toothbrush and toothpaste. Tuck into a little basket and tie with a ribbon for your guest bathroom.

∾ Other extras that will be appreciated: a travel iron and small ironing board, a hair dryer, a clothes brush, notepaper and pens, literature on local attractions. Why not treat your guests to a disposable camera, too?

∾ Basics can make a big difference to the experience of hospitality. Is there plenty of toilet paper in the bathroom your guests will use? Are there extra towels?

∾ Try putting an overnight guest in your child's room for the night and give your child the "privilege" of camping out in the living room. The result: an adventure for your child and welcome privacy for your guest.

- If your guest is an old friend, pull out a picture of the two of you together, tuck it into an antique frame, and place it on the bedside table.

- Even if guests elect to stay in a nearby motel, you can extend hospitality with a few special touches. Have a floral arrangement sent to their room. Or leave a basket of homemade muffins at the desk for their arrival.

- It's a thoughtful gesture to ask in advance about your guests' needs: allergies, physical limitations, or other special circumstances. The most beautiful home can lose its welcoming ambience if vegetarians are served meat, allergic people are obliged to sleep with the cat, or guests with arthritic needs must climb stairs three times a day.

- When other people extend hospitality to you, don't forget to thank them! A heartfelt note or a little gift will let your hosts know how much you appreciate them. And a return invitation should be not an obligation, but a joy.

But every house where Love abides
And Friendship is a guest,
Is surely home, and home, sweet home;
For there the heart can rest.

—HENRY VAN DYKE

Always a Place to Play

A HOUSE THAT WELCOMES CHILDREN

I don't believe in childproofing my home.

To me, that sounds as if children and homes are natural enemies—as if they need to be protected from one another.

And I just don't believe that's true. At least, that has never been true for me—and at one time in my life our house was home for five children under six years of age!

Even today, our nest is far from empty as far as children are concerned. Our five grandchildren and their friends are frequent visitors. Other children come with their parents for one reason or another. And I've never felt that I had to make my house "proof" against any of these small guests. Instead,

*God looks down
well pleased
to mark
In earth's dusk
each rosy spark,
Lights of home
and lights of love,
And the child the
heart thereof.*

— KATHERINE TYNAN

I want them to feel a part of everything we're doing. They add an incredible richness and vitality to our lives and to our home by helping to make it a friendly and welcoming place to be.

Yes, of course, we make provisions for keeping curious little ones safe. We cover our electric plugs and keep our household poisons in high cabinets. If there is the slightest chance that small children will enter the doors of any home, I think we owe it to our conscience to make the house safe for them.

It's not the concept of home safety that I object to, but the sound of the term *childproofing*.

What I want is a house that is not childproof but child-friendly.

When I establish a household where children feel welcome, where they feel free to be children, where they find furnishings and activities suitable for them and yet feel included in the overall life of the household—and where they are kept safe from household hazards—I believe my home feels more welcoming to children and adults alike.

Do you know what's the nicest benefit of making our home child-friendly?

I find it also makes our house more friendly to the child within me.

When I surround myself with childlike things—with vintage toys and lovely dolls and whimsical books—I find that my spirit stays fresher, more playful, more spontaneous and loving.

The child in me is comforted by the presence of teddy bears and rag dolls and little wooden trucks and miniature tea sets.

My whole life is not only richer but more lighthearted, more comforted. I feel safer and more protected when I infuse my home with a childlike spirit.

So a child-friendly house is not just a gift to the children who live there, the children who visit, and to their parents. It's a gift to anyone who visits—a sign that this is a house where the whole person is nurtured, even the child within.

It's a place where you can learn, a place where you can make mistakes and be forgiven.

It's a place where you can explore, where you can share, where you can always find something that is just your size in a world that often feels too big.

It's a place to pretend, a place where imagination and creativity flourish.

It's a place to work.

But always, always, there's a place to play.

That's the kind of house that welcomes children of all ages—the kind of house that always feels delightfully at-home.

Equipping a Home to Be Child-Friendly

What does it take to make a home child-friendly?

At the most basic level, it begins with remembering what it's like to be a child and what children like. Children love to pretend and imagine and create. They love being able to have adventures within safe limits. They respond to beauty with enthusiasm and learn with gusto, especially if the learning is accompanied with praise and a sense of accomplishment.

And, of course, every child loves toys—the tools with which they imagine and grow and learn. The most basic way to establish a child-friendly atmosphere in any home is to keep a few (or many) classic, time-proven toys in a place where every child can find them.

My friend Anne remembers an old washstand on her grandmother's screened-in porch that always held a set of blocks, some crayons, and a can of pickup sticks. Whenever they would visit, the grandchildren knew where to go for those games—and they understood to pick them up and put them away when play was over. Now Anne's daughter, Elizabeth, and her little cousins also know the secret of the toys on Great grandma's porch.

Our home contains several toy centers like that one, and visiting children nose them out with unerring instinct. Most of the toys and games are upstairs in our loft, but a little stash waits in a fabric-covered box under a bench in our breakfast room, ready for fireside play.

Boxed games are stacked on a low shelf in a nearby closet. Children's books live on a low shelf of the Princess Room, where adult guests as well as children enjoy their delightful texts and rich illustrations. Dollies and bears and other fuzzy friends reside in every room—perched on a window seat, cuddled against a cushion, comfortably ensconced in a child-sized rocker—always ready for a gentle hug.

And I always try to keep an emergency box on hand with quiet activities to amuse a child who might happen to accompany her mother on a visit. I maintain a supply of crayons, coloring books, simple games, and books for all ages. I also like to keep a supply of small gifts—barrettes, stickers, little flashlights—to send home. And I always keep juice in the refrigerator and peanut butter in the pantry—dependable, child-friendly snacks.

If children are permanent residents in your home, of course, they will have their own playthings, and each toy will have a permanent home. Learning to manage belongings and personal living space is an important part of learning to make oneself at home, and a simple, clear system for storing toys and belongings is vital to any child-friendly home.

It doesn't take much, really, to equip your home to be child-friendly. And doing so certainly doesn't need to be expensive. Wonderful, usable toys can be found at garage sales, thrift shops, and discount stores, or in your attic. Even at retail price, classic toys such as dominoes, blocks, and cuddly stuffed animals are remarkably inexpensive.

And some of the best playthings are not really toys at all. Your old clothing and jewelry can stock a dress-up box. A basket of used cereal boxes and margarine tins is perfect for playing store. Some crayons, a stack of paper, and some scissors can occupy a child for hours. And as any parent of small children has learned on Christmas morning, a simple cardboard box can provide endless amusement.

If you are in doubt about how to equip your child-friendly home, invite a child to advise you. And if you have no access to young advisers, then buy what you like. Buy what tickles your memories, what triggers warm, cozy feelings, what tempts you to get down on the floor and play. Buy something that makes you happy, and then look for a child to share it.

Child-sized Spaces

In addition to toys, children like spaces and furniture that are just their size. Automatically they gravitate to cozy little caves and scaled-down nooks in which they can curl up and play. If there are secret spaces or hidey-holes, all the better.

The child in me immediately said, "Aha" when I saw the tidy little loft above our kitchen and entryway. I knew that wonderful little space would be a perfect child headquarters for our house. Our children by that time were grown and out of the nest, but grandchildren were on the way. So with imagination and some sheets that were on sale, Jenny and I worked to create a dream playhouse that would serve first for baby Christine and then for every grandchild and child visitor who came along.

The sheets became a crib set (we've left the crib up since there always seems to be a baby around), matching curtains, and a tufted wall covering behind the built-in captain's bed. Then the tiny peach roses in the sheets became inspiration for a stenciled design that circled the whitewashed floors and happily climbed the walls.

From there we simply added hand-me-down furniture and some play-day basics: a child-sized table and chairs, a wicker cradle full of baby dolls, shelves full of games and stuffed animals, and a giant-sized Winnie the Pooh to keep an eye on things.

I've yet to meet a child who could resist our loft. Some days I can barely resist it myself. That loft has been a tea room, a game room, a hospital (both pretend and real), and a reading nook. Because we keep the closet full of dress-up clothes, from my old nighties to Bob's cast-off neckties, it is also "drama central." I'll never forget the day our Chad came downstairs decked out in my old blazer and a necktie from the dress-up closet and carrying a Bible. He announced in solemn tones that he was now a preacher!

But you don't even have to build a separate room just to establish a child-friendly space in your home. A couple of child-sized rocking chairs in a cozy corner next to a basket of books will do it. So will a beanbag chair on a rug by the fire with a checkerboard hanging on the wall. And there's always the time-tested option of a couple of blankets draped over a card table to create a cozy and welcoming nest. Very few children can resist that kind of a small, dark cave. On a really hectic day, you may find yourself crawling in as well.

Wide, Open Spaces

The outdoors is a child's native habitat, and most children are out the door the minute the opportunity presents itself. Even a tiny yard can provide any child with a place to explore and have fun.

For most children, the star attraction of our house and grounds is our tree house. This simple platform, which surrounds our big ash tree like a Swiss Family Robinson habitat, has been the center of countless games and parties, from a Desert Storm cookout to a dainty tea party to a rollicking rock-and-roll dance party. (This last took place during the reception of Brad and Maria's wedding!)

Our tree house isn't fancy, and it didn't really cost much. It's just a platform surrounded by ropes for safety and accessed by a plain wood ladder. Beneath it is our chicken coop—another star attraction for animal-loving youngsters.

It doesn't take much to provide an outdoor welcome for children. All they really need is raw materials for their imagination.

A mattress box rescued from the recycling bin will provide any child with hours of fun.

A few sturdy plastic yard toys from a

garage sale will say to a child, "I care about you, too."

Or why not outfit a small visitor with a shovel and show where he or she can dig in the garden?

Better yet, put on your gardening togs and invite a child to come work with you. As you do, you will be establishing another vital element of a child-friendly home: You will be establishing a space where the generations live and work and learn together and where one generation can teach another what it means to establish strong, warm, welcoming households.

Homes, you see, are learning labs for "at-homeness." They are where children learn both by teaching and example what it means to take care of themselves and other people. A welcoming home is an ideal teaching space where a child can learn not only social graces, but also the dynamics of working and living with others.

A child who participates in the life of the home learns to be part of a family. A child who grows up in a homey, welcoming home learns how to make herself and other people at home. A child who helps take responsibility for these things in early years learns to take responsibility as she grows.

Yours, Mine, and Ours

In our home, we have always assigned home responsibilities according to the "yours, mine, and ours" principle.

Each person in a household, for instance, needs some personal, private "yours" space. Depending on the household, this may be a bedroom and bath, part of a room, or just a bed and a footlocker, but it is yours to decorate and organize as you see fit. If you want to hang horse posters or athletic pennants on your bedroom walls or paint your personal bathroom yellow and black, that's your decision (even if it doesn't

go with my lovely country-eclectic decor). But you also have the responsibility to keep it clean and organized. When you are little, I will help you and teach you how to do this: how to make the bed, to put away belongings, to establish a place for everything. But as you grow, the goal will be for you to take responsibility for doing these things yourself.

Of course, there are also parts of the household that are mine: my private space, my belongings, and my responsibility. This may be my bedroom and bath and perhaps

an office or work space. It's part of my job to model for you in these areas how I can take care of my own belongings and my own space and make these personal areas comfortable and homey.

And then there are the "ours" areas: the living room, the family room, the kitchen, and the utility room. A playroom or a bedroom and bath may be shared among children in a household, or a single bathroom may serve the entire family. These "ours" areas are everyone's responsibility. Everyone has a say in how they are decorated and arranged. And I believe that in these areas there should be a space for everyone to be comfortable and to participate, even the smallest child.

This may mean setting up child-sized tables and chairs in a corner of the breakfast room or using booster seats in the dining room. It may mean a toy box in the corner of the living room or an array of children's books on the bottom shelf in the family room.

But it also means that the knickknacks and objects that the parents enjoy are out in the open, not stored away. A child-friendly house should not be one where adults' needs are ignored! There are magazines on the coffee table, lamps on the side table, plants in the corner. In my case, there are bone-china teacups on open shelves and even on small carts within arm's reach of small explorers.

To me, this is all part of the learning process. I wanted my children, and I want my grandchildren, to experience the joy of living among beautiful things and to learn to care for those things. In my experience, even very young children can learn this lesson happily and proudly—especially when they are introduced to the treasures under supervision, allowed to touch and admire, then provided with age-appropriate toys and a place where they can play.

Yes, I do have a few treasured pieces that go on the higher shelves, and I try to supervise the visits to my special shelves. I always stress to little ones that some objects can break and need to be handled carefully. But I always stress that I know accidents can happen and that if one of these treasures should break, it's all right, because the children who come to my house are far more precious than any piece of china or glass.

I believe that to the bottom of my heart.

To me, the real treasures of any home are the people of all sizes who are growing, creating, playing, sharing, and learning there. These are the treasures that truly make a house a home.

The Chain of Memory

Another vital teaching function of a child-friendly home is the transmission of values and traditions from one generation to the next. In fact, this is one of the prime purposes for establishing a home in the first place.

When I am serving a tea party to my granddaughter and grandsons (and we have had tea together since they were very small), I am passing on to them the things my mama passed on to me: the value of manners, the power of beauty in small rituals, the joy of spending quiet time together.

When Bob reads Bible stories to our grandchildren or works with them in our garden, he is passing along the treasures his family gave him: a deep faith, a love of growing things, a respect for hard work.

When we all participate together in family gatherings and traditions—decorating the Christmas tree, watching slides and family videos, playing board games, working on crafts, or just telling stories and sharing remembrances—we are building a chain of memories that will stretch unbroken into the future.

And as we interact with these children and include them in our work and play, we are teaching them what it means to be healthy adult men and women—strong and loving, hardworking and relaxed, cooperative and independent, living together with others in harmony and integrity.

These are not lessons that can be taught through a lecture.

They are lessons that are caught through the way we live.

And that is the essence of why I think a child-friendly home is vital both to our own happiness and to the happiness of future generations.

This lesson was brought home to me with special poignance the other day when I overheard my just-turned-teenager granddaughter Christine playing with her little cousin Westin in the loft. She had pulled out the Red-Riding-Hood storytelling doll. It's a two-headed doll. You flip it one way and it's Red Riding Hood. Turn the cape around, and it's the grandmother. And flip the whole thing over, and it's the big, bad wolf! I have used the doll many times to tell that wonderful old story to Christine and her brothers. But I knew the chain of tradition and memory was adding links when I heard Christine telling the same story to her little cousin—turning and flipping the same doll as she spoke.

That forging of the memory chain, that continuation of tradition is such a vital part of any homey, welcoming home. What we teach our children—or any child who shares our lives—they will teach their children. What we share with our children, they will share with generations to come.

And if we share with them a child-friendly home, they will learn to establish a comfortable, welcoming home for generations to come.

HOUSEWARMINGS

IDEAS FOR CHILD-FRIENDLY SPACES

- Children love to play with "real stuff." Instead of policing children around your tools and treasures, offer them tools and treasures of their own and supervise as necessary. All our grandsons are proud owners of Swiss army knives, kept safely at our house and used only when Papa Bob and I are nearby.

- Most children appreciate beauty, and they love being treated like grown-ups. If a child comes to stay, why not put a vase of fresh flowers in his or her room?

- Children who visit us love to take their own little sack lunches (peanut butter and jelly, carrots, and apples) to the loft or the tree house while the grown-ups enjoy lunch downstairs.

- A source of child-spirited decorating treasure may be as close as your attic or your mother's attic. With a good dusting or perhaps a professional cleaning, a toy or doll or even a framed "blankie" from your childhood could become a wonderful conversation piece—and children will love to hear its story.

- Before you destine a piece of old clothing or jewelry for the garage-sale stack, stop and think: Would this work in a dress-up box? If you don't have children in your house often, consider donating dress-up clothes to a local day-care center.

- Old toys and miniatures picked up at thrift stores can be great for decorating. Tuck them in the corner of a shelf, or even use them for a centerpiece.

- Our friend Ellen has always "shopped" first in her children's rooms when looking for some special way to decorate for guests. A doll's blanket may become a table runner or a place mat, tiny metal trucks might hold place cards, or a stack of blocks can make a wonderful centerpiece.

- The secret of really good children's literature is that adults love it, too—plus many of today's children's books are beautifully illustrated. So why not go shopping in the children's section when you're looking for a wonderful coffee-table book?

- Provide workable storage for all your "kid stuff" and encourage children to put things away. A big toy box is usually not the best solution—a tangle of unrelated toys is no fun to play with. Shelves are a better bet. I like to cover file-sized boxes with fabric to store different kinds of playthings: puzzles in one, dress-up clothes in another.

- Child-sized chairs, rocking chairs, and step stools—when they're not doing their regular duty—are wonderful places to display your other treasures. One of my favorite ways to welcome guests is a rag doll sitting by the door in her chair with a little welcome sign in her lap.

- Children's items make wonderful collectibles. Along with my "grown-up" teacup collection, I've enjoyed collecting miniature children's tea sets as well. I also collect rag dolls and children's books. Think back on your own childhood. What was your favorite toy? That memory could be the start of a fascinating collection.

- Playing children's games can help adults let down their hair, too. When children come to visit, why not have a time when everyone can play games like tag, hide-and-seek, capture the flag, and kick the can. Modify the rules, if you have to, so that all ages can join in—and remember to have fun.

Thus, simply as a little child, we learn a home is made from love.
Warm as the golden hearthfire on the floor. . . .
— ANONYMOUS

The Fun of Alfresco

BRINGING THE OUTDOORS IN AND THE INDOORS OUT

I learned it many years ago. I am a better person, a happier person, when I am in close daily contact with the outdoors.

Sunshine, flowers, a fresh breeze, something green—all these outdoor blessings help keep my feet on the ground and my spirits high. And I always feel more at home in my house when I am able to bring a touch of the outdoors into our home—or, even better, to make the outdoors a part of our home.

I've felt that way ever since I was a little girl, and I'll bet you have, too. Remember the days when morning shot you out of the house like a cannon, eager to spend as many hours as possi-ble in the sunshine? Remember running through sprinklers and digging in the dirt and begging your mother for a picnic?

You felt that way because you were made that way. I truly believe we humans were designed to crave the outdoors and to yearn for outdoor living. For most of us, food tastes better, friendship feels warmer, days seem a little brighter, when we are living alfresco.

Alfresco—that's the Italian word for "outdoors." But the literal meaning of the word is even more inviting. *Alfresco* actually means "in the cool" or "in the freshness." And doesn't that sound like a delicious, delightful place to be?

Light is sweet, and it pleases the eyes to see the sun.

—ECCLESIASTES 1:9

Living Alfresco

In the years since we bought our current house, we have gradually added to the number of places where we can enjoy a bit of alfresco enjoyment.

Our dining room, garden room, and offices all cluster around a cozy brick courtyard cooled by a trickling fountain. Potted plants of all descriptions tumble in green profusion. Across from our front door, a serene fish pond sparkles beside a little deck—a favorite family picnic spot.

Our cool veranda, shaded by movable awnings and the sparkling poplar trees that were a birthday present from Bob to me, is a lush place to read on a hot afternoon, an idyllic spot to enjoy a pasta dinner with friends. And Bob's garden, with its neat raised containers, its fruit trees, its rose arbors, is a delight for evening strolls with the grandchildren. So are the cinder paths that circle our property under the trees.

We love the outdoor ambience of our present home. But we were finding ways to enjoy alfresco living long before we had the room and the means to put in pools and paths. Ever since we began our life together, we have been finding ways to bring the outdoors into our home and to let our indoor life out into the outdoor freshness.

Our very first tiny apartment, remember, featured a wrought-iron picnic set for a dining table. We felt that we were having a picnic at every meal. Then, every time I would go out, I would bring home a pot of chrysanthemums or geraniums, which would then travel from table to bedside to windowsill—wherever we needed a touch of the outdoors. And whenever we could, we would take a basket, a blanket, and our dinner (which on our budget was usually very simple) and just sit outside to enjoy the food, the breeze, and the sunset.

Then we bought our first little tract home and began gardening. Bob comes from a farming family, but we still were learning together what it takes to build an outdoor paradise in a hot, dry climate. Right away, however, we created a little patio with an overhang so we could enjoy our meals outdoors.

In that first little home, we also decided to get creative in terms of bringing the outdoors in. We took a little front bedroom off our entry hall and put in bamboo straw matting, a water fountain, lots of ferns, and a little couch. We made a little lanai (a Hawaiian sitting room) out of that bedroom. I kept my sewing machine there, and we also put in a little table so we could enjoy indoor picnics.

Since that time, houses have come and gone. Children have been born and have grown up and left the nest. Our careers have changed. But that sense of wanting to live close to the outdoors has never left us.

We know that life isn't a picnic.

But we never ever want to live our lives without the possibility of a picnic—indoors or out. We have never felt truly at home unless the outdoors was part of our lives.

Bringing the Outdoors In

So how do you make yourself and others at home, alfresco?

I'd start with the very simplest ploy.

You can start with bringing the outdoors in.

If you can, open a window and let the fresh breeze play. Or at the very least, open the curtains and invite the sunshine indoors.

Windows allow the outdoors to smile into your living space. Whenever possible, give them room to shine instead of weighing them down with heavy drapes or elaborate window treatments.

If the view is good, open the curtains—or eliminate them entirely. If you need to keep out prying eyes or a blinding glare or a view of the neighbor's garbage cans, try translucent screens or blinds, or install a skylight. But whenever possible, let in a little sunshine to help your interior smile.

Houseplants are also a wonderful way to bring the outdoors in. They are naturals for cleaning the air and refreshing the spirit, and there's a houseplant suitable for every shade of green thumb.

Our houseplants have always been happy nomads, traveling constantly from tabletop to hearth to windowsill and back outside again. The pots of herbs on my windowsill have been known to decorate a dinner table, adding delicious fragrance as well as a touch of outdoor greenery. A collection of pots on the patio have moved inside to liven up a summer fireplace. Cuttings of ivy from outside our bedroom have rooted themselves in a jar on the breakfast table.

You don't even need living plants, though, to give that indoor-outdoor feeling to your home. Floral fabrics and botanical prints, for instance, can make the darkest interiors bloom. I love fabrics printed with ivy, roses, violets, and mischievous little pansies (my favorites).

And thanks to my daughter, Jenny, and her creative decorator's eye, silk flowers and plants bloom in profusion throughout my house: atop dressers and mirrors, in bowls and pots, on wreaths. Bob's garden books and our seed catalogs tantalize us with their beautiful color pictures and spin their garden dreams on even the darkest winter days. Birdhouses perched on shelves and in corners add a whimsical woodland touch.

And whenever we go for a walk outdoors, either around our property or down the street, we try to pick up a little something for the house: a little spray of orange blossoms, a rose, a handful of reeds from around the pond, even a small branch from a blooming tree.

Our friend Ellen, who is a wonderfully creative decorator, even makes a point of taking a nature walk on the morning or afternoon of a dinner party, searching specially for beautiful natural objects to use as centerpieces and decorative items.

You don't even need vases. A lace table runner spread with collected leaves and nuts, Christmas greenery, or even an array of summer flowers can be a stunning centerpiece. If you arrange it just before the meal, the flowers will last, as will the impression of bountiful beauty. A few votive candles carefully tucked among the leaves and blossoms will add an unforgettable warmth.

Gifts from the Garden

One of my very favorite ways of bringing the outdoors in is to gather in the fruits of our garden.

What a joy to carry in an apronful of fresh greens, tomatoes, lemons, or avocados, to wash them and slice them and then taste their sunny freshness.

What a thrill to bring in a single rose or a basket of daisies, trim their stems, and give them a new home in a crystal vase.

And what a privilege to have participated in the growth of these beautiful outdoor things.

I am fortunate to be married to an accomplished and dedicated gardener, and the fruit of his planning and labor enriches the life of our whole family. Ever since Bob and I married, we have had a garden of some sort, even if it was only a few plants on the windowsill. Now we enjoy corn, onions, tomatoes, green beans, and more from Bob's carefully tended container gardens.

But you don't have to be a gardener on a large scale to have the pleasure of bringing in food from the outdoors. Even a foot-square plot by the porch planted in tulips or peppers can yield a surprising harvest. A single tomato plant in a tub on the patio can keep you in fresh vegetables all summer. A pot of herbs on the windowsill can flavor your food and your outlook.

And you don't even have to grow any of it yourself if you don't want to, or if circumstances forbid. You can help your local farmers and help yourself as well by seeking out farmers' markets, fruit stands, and other sources of homegrown produce.

One family I know that lives in Minnesota has made apple-picking an annual ritual. Mother, father, and the two little girls go out together to a local orchard and work together to pick a bushel. After a day in the crisp autumn air, they make their way home to enjoy, literally, the "fruit of their labors." Not only do they feast for months on wonderful crisp apples and homemade applesauce, apple pie, and apple jelly, but they also enjoy the sight of the beautiful green and red fruit piled in baskets around their kitchen, outdoor sweetness beautifully adorning their lives.

Bringing the Indoors Out

But the outdoors is so much more than a source of food and decorating material. For me, at least, the outdoors has always been its own reward.

When I was growing up, it seemed that all my fun was outdoors. Every summer day, as soon as my chores were done and the Murphy bed where Mama and I slept was back in the wall, I would meet my best girlfriend and we would be off to the beach or the park on our bicycles. I would leave dinner slow-cooking in the oven (those were the days before Crockpots) and return just in time to get it on the table. The bulk of the day would be spent outdoors in the sun and the fresh air.

These days, I rarely have a full day to enjoy outdoors, but I relish my morning walks along the irrigation canal in Riverside, enjoying the company of other walkers, the morning air, the sweet smell of orange blossoms, the bright freshness of bougainvillea, and the gentle flow of the water beside me.

On the days I miss my walk, I always feel I've missed much more than the exercise. So I take whatever opportunity I can to at least take a spin through the garden or sit out on the patio to get a little touch of sun on my face and wind in my hair. Sometimes I'll just take a glass of lemonade out and sit in one of the lawn chairs. Sometimes I'll even nap on the veranda, lulled to sleep by the trickling of the fountain. Or I'll take my book or my journal out under the trees for a quiet time of reading or meditation.

And this, of course, is the other side of living in close contact with the outdoors. Not only can we bring the outdoors in, but we can also bring our indoor selves outside, enjoying our everyday activities in the open air.

Meals alfresco, for example, are always a wonderful treat. And Bob and I try not to miss an opportunity to enjoy our meals in the open air.

Mornings when the weather is good, we inevitably end up on the patio or the veranda with our orange juice and cereal and coffee.

Lunchtime is often a picnic, with a card table set up by the pond or carried in a basket to a local park. Dinner is likely to include chicken breasts grilled on the veranda, with a big salad from the garden and a loaf of crusty French bread. And anytime is a good time for a bowl of chips with fresh salsa or just a glass of lemonade out where the weather is nice.

Occasionally I'll even pack a "love basket"—complete with wonderful food, something to drink, china, candles, and a vase for flowers—so we can take an entire meal wherever the spirit moves us. Once Bob and I even enjoyed a love-basket picnic in the tree house—what a romantic time!

Furnishing Your Outdoor Life

If you are lucky enough to have a large porch, patio, or deck, your options for inside-out living are many. We have never regretted the outdoor areas we have constructed; in fact, we seem to spend more and more time in these places every year. But you don't have to spend a fortune on decking and lawn furniture to enjoy an alfresco life.

You can sit on the stoop to watch the world go by or spread a blanket in the grass to look at the stars.

You can fire up a hibachi on the balcony

or just lean over the railing to enjoy the sunrise.

You can invite an office acquaintance to share a picnic on a park bench or enjoy a cup of coffee at a sidewalk café.

Or you can just take your indoor life out on the lawn for a little while. There's no law that says you can't!

Weather and doorways permitting, your chairs and tables and footstools and—who knows?—even your sofa might enjoy getting outdoors for a bit.

Your quilts can cuddle you just as warmly under a tree as in a window seat. Your antique china or linens can be handled just as carefully on a quiet picnic as they would be at a dinner party. Your pillows will be as comfy in a hammock as on your bed.

In fact, even if you do have a patio or a deck or a lavish sun porch, you can still have some fun by bringing these indoor friends outside from time to time for a bit of fresh air.

If you find that you enjoy this kind of indoor-outdoor living, you might want to invest in furniture that makes it all a little easier.

Wicker is traditional and delightful for front porches and other outdoor spaces that are protected from the rain.

A porch swing or lawn swing is guaranteed to bring out the child in anyone, and an hour or so of quiet rocking at twilight, while fireflies flicker and children play nearby, can easily transport you to earlier, less-stressful times.

Bob and I love the versatility and comfort of molded plastic lounges and chairs; these are weather-hardy, easily portable, and very affordable. But we also enjoy the sturdiness of an iron table and permanent chairs.

Some form of protection from the elements can extend the possibilities for outdoor living. In our sunny climate, we are especially grateful for the movable awnings that can be positioned to provide a shady bower on the hottest days. And of course, our trees provide the same welcome shelter. In a rainier climate, a porch or a roofed patio can enable indoor-outdoor living even on rainy days, and a portable heater or a patio fireplace can render chilly days not only comfortable, but delightful.

And when the weather simply won't permit an outdoor sojourn, the outdoor celebration can move indoors once more.

A cool salad of homegrown tomatoes and basil with lemonade while the sun beats down outside.

A sunny bouquet on a rainy autumn afternoon.

A dreamy hour in a comfortable chair with a catalog full of roses.

Indoors or out, it's the freshest, most lovely way to make a house a home.

Housewarmings

- One of the easiest ways to have hospitality and fellowship alfresco is to take your guests on a walk. Stroll around the neighborhood after dinner for quiet talk and fresh air.

- Garden and lawn furniture can make adorable indoor furniture as well. Have you considered a redwood picnic table for a breakfast nook? Or why not hang a bright-colored hammock in the corner of the family room?

- Don't overlook gardening tools and decorations as decorating possibilities. A simple, inexpensive terra-cotta pot, painted or plain, can hold toothbrushes, candles, potpourri, or even a plant! A small cement animal, meant for the garden, can lurk delightfully in the corner of a bathroom. Or how about a sundial at the end of a sofa for holding drinks or magazines?

- Fresh flowers are the best way I know to bring the outdoors in. Whether they come from a florist, the local grocery store, or your own garden, try to keep them around. And don't worry too much about elaborate arrangements. When a professional decorator came to our house for a photo shoot, I was surprised to see her just plop ready-made bouquets into big vases. A few pulls and tugs, and she was through. The effect was simple and fresh.

- Picnics are the original form of alfresco dining, and they are wonderfully versatile sources of fun. You can carry it all in a plastic bag, but why not invest in a sturdy picnic basket or hamper? Then use your imagination. Why not try a picnic on the grounds of an art museum, at the train station, on a friend's lawn? Or place all your potted plants in a circle and picnic in your living room!

- If you are lucky enough to have a room that receives lots of morning sunshine, turn it into a sun room. Decorate with wicker or outdoor furniture, plenty of comfortable cushions, and houseplants everywhere.

- Send for every plant catalog you read about. It's an easy way to learn the names of flowers and a great opportunity to see them in color. And browsing through the bright catalogs can bring springtime indoors even on a dreary winter day.

- Did you ever grow a sweet-potato garden as a child? Get a quart-sized jar and a sweet potato and try again. (All you have to do is stick the potato in water and wait for a windowful of lovely heart-shaped leaves.) Better yet, share the fun of growing a potato with your favorite child.

- Old windows make wonderful lawn and garden decorations. You can get them from wreckers, construction firms, and certain architectural antique firms. We have one hanging by chains from one wall of our patio and another, made from stained glass, hanging from a lattice colonnade.

- To protect an area of your house or garden from the harsh sun, plant an arbor. Set up a frame of latticework (or even strings) and train ivy or morning glories or other climbing plants along it. Soon you will have a leafy green "curtain" to keep you cool—and perhaps flowers to boot.

- Ivy makes an inexpensive, wonderfully fresh decorating tool. Try weaving lengths of English ivy into circlets to serve as wreaths, candleholders, or even napkin rings. Or for a festive and traditional Christmas table, combine sprays of holly and ivy down the center. Decorate with tartan bows and tiny white votive candles in clear glass holders.

Oh, how good everything tasted in that bower,
with the fresh wind rustling the poplar leaves, sunshine and
sweet wood-smells about them, and birds singing overhead.

—SUSAN COOLEDGE

The Business of Living

CREATING A HOSPITABLE WORK SPACE

I truly love the idea of my house being a respite, a cozy bed-and-breakfast experience for people who visit us.

But we're not on vacation when we live here!

This is not a summer home where our primary activity is lounging on the patio or popping burgers on the grill. Our home is a place where the real work of living goes on—and I believe that's true for every at-home home. Clothes are cleaned, folded, and mended. Meals are prepared. Packages are wrapped. Toilets are scrubbed. Flowers are arranged.

Increasingly, too, our home is where the work of making a living goes on. Like growing numbers of people, Bob and I maintain a home-based business. Here is

The homeliest tasks get beautiful if loving hands do them.

—**LOUISA MAY ALCOTT**

where we make calls, send faxes, prepare seminars, and write books.

And other people come to work in our house as well. A wonderful woman named Sally helps me clean my house (and also occasionally brings us a pumpkin pie). Our friend Ellen keeps on top of our mail orders and makes herself invaluable around our business (as well as supplying creative ideas for my books). So does our friend Sherry, who delivers typed manuscripts and disks from her own home-based business. Occasionally my editors or publishing friends come to call.

Your circumstances are probably different, but chances are that your house, too, is a working house.

Think about it.

Your home is a hospital, where splinters are removed and "boo-boos" are bandaged.

It's a mailing and wrapping center, where packages are prepared and sent.

It's an office, where bills are paid and letters are written.

It's a child-development center, where the next generation is nurtured and trained.

All this means that in a truly welcoming and inviting home, some thought needs to be given to where and how that work will be done. You need a place and a plan for making, fixing, cleaning, and creating things—and for feeling joyfully at home in the process.

For me, that doesn't mean a stark beige-and-gray "office" hiding behind closed doors. And it doesn't mean a cluttered corner of the garage where Bob has his workshop. Neither does it have to mean an expensive room dedicated to crafts or sewing or woodworking or whatever.

It simply means a comfortable and efficient spot for carrying on the business of living.

A separate room for work is a wonderful luxury, but a lap desk and a set of baskets or a hidden bookshelf or a big box under the bed will do the trick.

The kitchen, of course, is the dedicated workroom for the business of making food, conversation, and camaraderie. And in our kitchen, we have a kind of "command center" with a phone, a message board, an address book, and pictures of the grandchildren.

But we have several other areas in our home that beckon us to do what needs to be done with a joyous and willing spirit.

A Welcoming Work Space

Because our business is based at home, Bob and I both maintain home offices. Mine is tucked into a corner of what used to be our seminar room and now has become our airy garden room. Bob's is across the patio from mine, around a corner in the breezeway—a former utility room that we carpeted and furnished to become a comfortable work space.

My office contains copies and keepsakes, books and photos—and, of course, a phone and fax. It occupies its own discrete corner, but it overlooks a comfortable and lovely sitting area, and I can gaze out through the French doors onto the patio while I talk on the phone to set up seminars or dream about what to write next.

Bob's office is comfortably masculine,

with a big oak desk, rich-colored wallpaper, and lots of books. This is where he takes care of our business finances and does his own writing.

In addition to our offices, we also are blessed to have a room for taking care of some of the nuts-and-bolts tasks that go with running a home. Our utility room off the breezeway holds the washer and dryer, the ironing board, the sewing machine, and a miscellany of supplies for cleaning and crafting. A big pull-out drawer collects small gifts for impromptu giving— picked up whenever I browse an antique store or flea market. And a stand-up wrapping-paper organizer (holding paper, tape, scissors, and ribbon) allows me to wrap up those little tokens in style, with a minimum of fuss.

These dedicated work areas are dreams come true to me, true luxuries, and I am grateful for them because I haven't always had such set-aside space for office work and housework and crafts.

I spent many years with my work supplies in cardboard boxes, the portable sewing machine tucked away in a closet (and clothes cut out on the kitchen table), the ironing board hung behind a door, and my "office" composed of a card table and metal shelves in the garage. And while certainly not luxurious, these simple and basic setups did their job! The same principles that help me organize my work space now helped me work comfortably in less-than-ideal circumstances.

Working in Beauty

The trick, I have come to believe, is to be as organized as possible without being rigid, to let your work fit naturally in your home and the fabric of your day but not to let it take over, and to remember that beauty is as necessary in the places where you do your work as it is in the places where you talk and

sleep and play.

It may be *more* necessary, in fact.

I truly believe that work, even the sometimes-tedious work of keeping a home, was meant to be a joy, not a burden. It is the place where our creativity shines, where we garner the fun of achievement. Why can't we make our work spaces as comfortable and welcoming as we do our rest places?

I don't mean we have to put little ruffled skirts on our fax machines or paint all our mop buckets to match the wallpaper. But it's just as easy to buy (or make) a cheerfully printed ironing-board cover as a plain gray one. It's not all that time-consuming to cover cardboard storage boxes with contact paper or fabric. Even a battered old desk looks better with some family photos and a little vase of flowers on it.

And why not hang pictures in the utility room?

When Bob first did that, I was surprised and a little shocked. It had never occurred to me to actually decorate the room where I did the laundry. But I found that I liked having something nice to look at when I was doing wash or folding clothes or ironing. Soon we got into the habit of hanging little extra decorations—plaques, pictures, even colorful advertisements—in the utility room, and now we have almost a little gallery. I've sewn matching covers for my ironing board and sewing machine, set up a system of white plastic bins to hold my rags and other supplies, and the room is a cozy, comfortable place to work.

In my actual office, I find that a beautiful work space is absolutely essential to maintaining a willing spirit. After all, if the rest of the house is cozy and inviting, why would I want to spend a lot of time in a spartan, mismatched area?

So I cover the walls with memorabilia, pepper the shelves with family photos as well as books, and gather plants around me. I use colorful file folders both to cheer me and keep me organized. We've just installed French doors behind my desk to open onto a tiny deck. (The light and the breeze lift my spirits immeasurably.)

In addition, I find that it's important to furnish my office work space in a way that reminds me that my work matters, that it has a distinct and definite place in my life. Although I have done a lot of work on card tables and folding desks, I work much more comfortably and meaningfully with a "real" desk. A supportive, "ergonomic" chair is absolutely necessary to making me feel welcome in my own work space. So is adequate lighting.

This principle of taking work seriously but allowing it to be beautiful carries over into the work of running a household, too. I have always felt that having "real" tools for housework dignifies these very necessary and worthy tasks, as well as reducing the time it takes to do them. I use a squeegee for windows, an ostrich-feather duster for dusting, a professional-size mop and bucket. I borrow tools and techniques from professional housecleaners.

And yet I'm not "all business" when I'm doing housework. I like to have lovely music on the stereo while I'm doing my work, and I like to use my housework time as a time to enjoy the comfort and beauty that surrounds me in my home. Then, when I'm through, I can tuck my tools away in their proper place in the utility room and enjoy the increased comfort and beauty that comes from carefully tending my nest.

A Welcome for All Workers

There are times, of course, that some of the jobs of keeping a house need to be turned over to someone else. But here, too, the spirit of welcome can be extended.

In recent years, as my speaking career has escalated, I have come to rely implicitly on the people who come to our house to help us run our home and our business. It has been a goal of ours to make these people feel comfortable and at home in our house, which, after all, is their work space for at least a short time.

If I'm home when these wonderful helpers are doing their jobs, I usually try to offer them lunch or at least a glass of iced tea. I try to pick up after myself so that the people who help me can concentrate on what they are hired to do. I try to write notes of appreciation along with instructions. (The appreciation is truly heartfelt!)

I believe that considerations like these are not beside the point when it comes to having a welcoming home. The workers in my home are there for a specific purpose, and I expect them to do their jobs, but I truly hope they will be blessed by the same coziness and at-home feeling that I enjoy in our house. I want their work space to be comfortable and inspiring, just as I want my work space to be.

A Welcoming Spot to Work

What kind of work goes on in your home? With just a little thought and planning, you can create a space that helps you do it with joy and enthusiasm.

I don't just mean maintenance chores or work-at-home jobs, either. I also am talking about labors of love: hobbies, crafts, avocations.

If you love to do calligraphy, you need a drawing board, a place to store pens and nibs, a good source of light, and a place to work where you won't be jostled.

If you dream of hand-carving a crèche set for each of your children, you need a place to store wood, an area where chips and curls of woods can be swept up easily, and a safe space to put away your sharp tools.

If knitting is your passion, you need a comfortable place to sit, an array of needles, a basket to hold that half-finished sweater, and a place to store all those balls and skeins of wonderful fiber that will someday be crafted into a work of wearable art.

And if you are going to write the great American novel, you need a computer, chair and desk and someplace to file research—or, at the very least, a good lamp and a place to store pencils and yellow writing pads.

How you fill these needs, of course, depends on your budget, your space, and your creativity. But no matter what your work, it seems, you need two things.

First, you need a comfortable place to do the work. For many kinds of pursuits, a place to work will mean a usable work surface: a desk, a shop table, or a drafting board. But it may simply be a comfortable chair next to a bright lamp. If possible, it should be permanent and "real"—a desk rather than a folding table, an office chair rather than one borrowed from the kitchen table, a drafting table or board instead of the breakfast bar, a small sewing-machine cabinet rather than the kitchen table. But I certainly wouldn't advise waiting for professional equipment before starting on a work you love. You can start where you are and go from there.

The amount you invest in a work space will depend on how much money you have to spend, how much space you can set aside, how much room the work demands, and how much time you plan to spend working there.

If you plan to work in a home office

eight hours a day, for instance, a chair and a desk that is the proper height for the work you do are not luxuries. A separate room or work area is essential for tax purposes.

If you are just learning to oil paint, however, you would probably not want to sink thousands of dollars into transforming the spare room into a studio with skylights, professional easel, and a sink for cleaning up. A folding table or easel, a portable paint box, and a small cabinet for storing supplies might be more appropriate—or just a craft box with a handle and a protective cover for the dining room table.

After all, you can always build a studio later.

Storage Solutions

A second thing you need in order to establish an at-home work space is storage. Adequate storage enables you to keep equipment and supplies readily at hand without their being in the way. Good storage also gives you a place to stow away your work in progress to give your eye and spirit time off.

Fortunately, creative solutions for storage abound in books and magazines, office supply stores, discount stores, hardware stores, and mail-order catalogs.

At one end of the spectrum are custom-built cabinets and bins.

At the other end are cardboard boxes rescued from the recycling bin and put to work in the interest of an organized and attractive work space.

In between are thousands of workable solutions for efficient, unobtrusive, even beautiful storage. An antique wardrobe or armoire can hold boxes of fabric scraps, a small quilting frame, quilting supplies, and a stack of completed quilts. A rustic-looking ammunition box can hold small tools. A refinished kitchen cabinet can store craft supplies, while an old picnic basket can conceal sketch pads and pencils. Shelves can be built in between wall studs or under a staircase.

The possibilities are limited only by your creativity.

One of my favorite pieces of furniture is an odd little cabinet I bought for 15 dollars at somebody's house many years ago. It's long and low, with doors in front. We now use it as a table behind our sofa, with a little lamp and an antique scale on top, but it also offers wonderful storage space. I use it as a kind of extra linen closet—a place to store tablecloths and napkins. It could also serve as an office credenza, a china cabinet, even a toy box.

Whenever Bob and I visit an antique store or a second-hand shop, we are on the lookout for such multipurpose pieces. Over the years, we've collected an oak icebox that now stores our crystal, a Hoosier cabinet that proudly displays teapots and teacups, a variety of wardrobes and bookcases that offer usable storage. We've also put inherited pieces—such as my mama's glass-front secretary—to use as storage pieces.

They all look so beautiful—who's to know that they are also helping the work of this household proceed smoothly and joyfully?

A Time and a Place

There is another side to making a home work space beautiful and inviting, however.

It needs to know its place.

A work place needs to be inviting and efficient and easy to access. It should invite you to pitch in and get things done. But then it should enable you to easily leave the work behind until the next session.

Even though you need a certain amount of inviting work space in your house, you don't want your entire home to be a work space. How can your home be a respite if everywhere you look you see nothing but tasks that need doing?

This can be a problem for people who earn their living from their homes. If not controlled, paperwork can migrate onto bedside tables, living room chairs, and kitchen counters. But this can also happen to hobby projects, to household equipment, and to unopened mail.

In order to keep a healthy balance between work and relaxation, there needs to be a way of dividing the two, of saying to yourself and the world, "I'm off-duty now."

If you have a separate work space, it may be as simple as shutting the door or putting up a screen.

If you are using the kitchen table, it may simply be a matter of putting the paintbrushes away and placing the canvases on a high shelf to dry.

If you live in a tiny efficiency apartment, it might mean turning off the computer, shutting off the desk light, filing the papers away, and going across the room to light a candle.

In any home, it's a matter of putting away the mop and the broom, putting the spray bottles back under the counter, and taking a deep, satisfied breath.

Work time is over. You've done it beautifully and joyfully, in a work space that welcomed you to the business of living.

Now, for the house and for yourself, it's time for a well-deserved rest.

Housewarmings

- Baskets are an inexpensive and beautiful solution to all manner of storage challenges. Haunt discount stores and import shops for big wicker baskets, little wall-hanging, partitioned baskets—whatever you can find. Hang them from your walls or ceilings or stack in the corner for a decorative accent that conceals a lot of storage.

- For maintenance chores that don't inherently warm your heart, make efficiency your goal. Invest in professional-quality cleaning equipment and supplies and learn to work quickly, leaving time for work you do love.

- Every home needs at least a minimal office space—a place to write letters, pay bills, and keep records. If you have no place for a desk, fill a storage box with office supplies and a lap desk and store in a closet or under a bed, preferably near a table and a telephone. When it's time to do your office work, simply pull out the box.

- A piece of plywood on two sawhorses makes a wonderful temporary space for cutting out clothes to sew or doing large craft projects. You can even create a padded surface by stapling blankets to the board. When you are through, the board and sawhorses can lean against a wall in your garage or even hide under a bed.

- As an alternative to hiding work supplies, try making them decorative. A large board with hooks for scissors, T-square, and so forth can make a striking graphic statement, especially if you mark the space for each item with a painted outline.

- Bookcases can hold more than books. Have you considered bookshelves to hold children's toys, sewing equipment, or office supplies? We have a glassed-in barrister's bookcase in our master bath to hold a variety of memorabilia.

- To hold pencils, pens, paintbrushes, knitting needles, or similar supplies try a colorful collection of coffee mugs lined up on a narrow shelf. Fill one of the mugs with an arrangement of dried flowers. You can do the same thing with a row of terra-cotta flowerpots.

- Keep gift-wrap paper together with bags, tissue paper, tape, ribbon, and scissors. I keep mine in an upright cardboard organizer, but plastic underbed containers are also available.

- File cabinets are wonderful solutions to paper clutter, and they don't have to be ugly. Did you know you can have your file cabinets painted to match your rooms? Or you can invest in an antique oak file cabinet. For a more inexpensive solution, hide the cabinet under a skirted table or use spray adhesive and cover an office-supply store file box with fabric.

- If storage space is tight, try decorating with items you would otherwise store. Stack bright quilts or pretty blankets under a lamp table or hang them on a stair rail. Pile costume jewelry into pretty antique containers on a dresser. Arrange hats or scarves on hooks on a wall.

- For a welcoming lift, share your work with a friend. Team up to clean both your houses—one house in the morning, one in the afternoon. Or meet together to sew, cook, or do crafts.

Let the most obvious eye catchers in any room be beautiful,
not utilitarian. You see not the ironing board, but a rose.

—ANNE ORTLUND

An Evolving Dream

When Bob and I first moved into the house where we now live, I was ecstatic. This was my dream house. I had been driving by it for years, long before the "For Sale" sign appeared on its lawn. I just knew it was the right place for us. And when by a series of miracles our offer was accepted and the financing arranged, I remember telling Bob, "You know what? This house is perfect. We won't have to do a thing to it."

I smile now when I remember that brash statement, because we've changed the house a lot! We've installed two Dutch doors and four or five sets of French ones. We have knocked out a kitchen wall to create a breakfast bar and installed glass fronts on all the cabinets. We have added two courtyards, a curving driveway, a fountain, a pool, a veranda, a garden, three rose arbors,

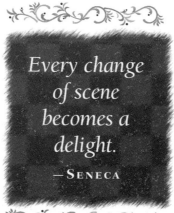

Every change of scene becomes a delight.
—SENECA

and countless trees. We've put in a pond and two barbecue grills. We've converted a utility room into an office. That's not even to mention the paint, the wallpaper, the chairs and beds and rugs and tables and decorative items that we have arranged and rearranged over the years.

This house is still our dream house. We still think it's perfect for us. But we know now that it will never be really finished. It will continue to grow and change as we grow and as our lives change.

And that's the way it's supposed to be. That's part of what makes us feel at home. Homes are not static monuments to taste. They're not museums. They are simply the stage where we experience the drama of our lives and where we invite others to share it with us. As the play changes, so will the set.

And the whole process, I believe, was meant to be fun.

I remember a time when I was collecting ducks. Ceramic ducks, concrete ducks, wooden ducks—all these graced my table-tops and nested in the corners of my house. I had duck magnets on the refrigerator. I wrote my notes on duck note paper. And I loved to tie little ribbons around the necks of my bigger pieces and set them out to welcome guests.

I remember thinking, "Oh, I love my ducks. I'm going to have these ducks around me always."

I was only partially right. Today, I'm not really interested in collecting ducks, and a great many of my beloved ducks have found new homes. A few of my favorites are still around, but even these old friends have moved graciously aside to make room for a growing collection of teacups and teapots and tea plaques and tea pillows.

My at-home dreams have evolved, in other words. My home has evolved along with them. And I have thoroughly enjoyed the process.

Our recently completed garden room is another example of the way a house can evolve. Its changing face has reflected the changes in our lives through the years since we moved in.

It came to us as a pool room, floored in concrete, complete with a jukebox. Because we had just started our More Hours in My Day business and were conducting seminars out of our home, we chose to convert that room into a seminar room. We set aside one corner to be my office, decorated the walls with whatever we could find, and invested in folding tables and chairs for the seminars. We also installed a brick courtyard outside to make the walk between house and seminar room more inviting for those who attended.

That office/seminar room served its purpose for many years. More recently, however, we realized that we were traveling more and more on the weekends and scheduling fewer and fewer seminars at home. We also realized that we wanted to reclaim that space for ourselves, to begin thinking toward a more private life.

Then we started dreaming about what that room could be. My office would still be there, of course, but what would we do with the extra space?

Perhaps it would be a library—a place where Bob could keep his growing collection of books. Or perhaps it could be a music room. I still dream of buying a cello and picking up lessons where I left off as a teenager.

But then we realized that we were gravitating more and more to that sunny courtyard and feeling more and more the need for a bright, light-filled living space. So we painted the whole room white, added French doors all around, installed a big, cozy fireplace and bookshelves, bought those big, cushy sofas, and created the office/sitting room where we all gather in the afternoons. We love to relax there in comfort while we gaze out toward the fountain and enjoy the cool breeze from the courtyard.

We are intensely pleased, in other words, with the way our new garden room has evolved.

But we can't promise this will be the final change!

A home is never really finished as long as living people fill it. Don't be afraid to change your home as your needs and priorities change. In fact, I think it's a good idea to keep thinking and planning ahead for change. I don't mean living in the chaos of constant construction or waiting a year to put up pictures in a new apartment. In fact, I think it's important to get a new space put together as quickly as possible, to put your personal touch on it and make it home.

But don't be compelled to have it all perfect or "finished." Leave room for something new. Experiment. Try out new ideas. You can always change them back! Get rid of items that don't work, and always be on the search for ideas that will make your living space more beautiful and welcoming.

But above all, think in terms of your evolving dreams. Think of a welcoming, relaxing haven that offers peace and beauty to everyone who comes inside, guest and visitor alike. Think of making yourself at home and then reaching out to make other people at home, too.

And then, by all means . . . dream on.

May the Lord give you the desire of your heart...
—PSALM 20:4